D0310263

THE QUEEN MOTHER REMEMBERED

The intimate recollections of her friends

1900–2002

Edited by James Hogg and Michael Mortimer

Published by BBC Books,
an imprint of BBC Worldwide Publishing,
BBC Worldwide Ltd, Woodlands,
80 Wood Lane, London W12 0TT
First published 2002

BBC Books would like to thank
the contributors for allowing their
interviews to be published.
ISBN 0 563 36214 6

Designed by Tim Higgins
Set in Monotype Lasercomp Garamond 156 by Butler & Tanner Ltd, Frome
Printed and bound in Great Britain by Butler & Tanner Ltd, Frome
Jacket printed by Lawrence Allen, Weston-super-Mare

The interviews which form the main section of this book took place in 1988, on the understanding that they would not be published during the Queen Mother's lifetime.

Most of the fifty-one people who agreed to talk about her had been her friends for many years. Given the circumstances of publication, they felt able to speak more freely than ever before about the character, and the place in history, of the woman who was always known among those close to her as Queen Elizabeth.

The Queen Mother in 1926, three years after becoming Duchess of York.

CONTENTS

Courtiers and Servants

Racing

Entertainment

The Castle of Mey

Politicians

CHRONOLOGY

1900	The Hon. Elizabeth Bowes Lyon born on 4 August, the ninth child of Lord and Lady Glamis.
1904	Father succeeds to the earldom of Strathmore, and she becomes Lady Elizabeth.
1914	First World War declared on her fourteenth birthday.
1915	One of her brothers, Fergus, killed in action.
1915–19	Glamis Castle, the Strathmores' Scottish home, serves as a convalescent hospital for soldiers. Lady Elizabeth spends the war looking after the wounded.
1920	George V makes his second son, Prince Albert, Duke of York. The Duke begins his courtship of Lady Elizabeth Bowes Lyon.
1923	She finally accepts the Duke of York's proposal of marriage, and their wedding takes place in Westminster Abbey on 26 April.
1926	Their first child, Princess Elizabeth, is born on 21 April.
1930	A second daughter, Princess Margaret, is born on 21 August.
1936	The death of George V brings his eldest son, Edward VIII, to the throne. Within months he abdicates to marry the divorced Mrs Simpson. The Duke and Duchess of York become King George VI and Queen Elizabeth.
1937	The Coronation takes place on 12 May.
1939	The King and Queen tour Canada and America in the spring. On 3 September war is declared against Germany.

Chronology

1940 The King and Queen narrowly escape injury when two bombs fall on Buckingham Palace, the first in a series of nine direct hits.

1945 On 8 May the Royal Family appear on the balcony of Buckingham Palace before jubilant crowds, to mark the end of the war in Europe.

1947 The King and Queen, with the two Princesses, tour South Africa. The tour is a success, but the King's health suffers. The heir to the throne, Princess Elizabeth, marries Prince Philip on 20 November.

1948 Silver Wedding anniversary of the King and Queen. Their first grandchild, Prince Charles, born on 14 November.

1949 The King is operated on for circulation problems.

1950 A second grandchild for the King and Queen, with the birth of Princess Anne on 15 August.

1951 The King's health deteriorates, and lung cancer is diagnosed.

1952 The King dies on 6 February.

1953 Coronation of Queen Elizabeth II. The Queen Mother buys the dilapidated Castle of Mey in Caithness. Princess Margaret falls in love with Group Captain Peter Townsend.

1955 Princess Margaret decides not to marry Group Captain Townsend.

1956 The Queen Mother's horse, Devon Loch, mysteriously falls in the finishing straight of the Grand National, when well in the lead.

1958 The Queen Mother becomes the first member of the Royal Family to fly round the world.

1960 Her third grandchild, Prince Andrew, born on 19 February. Princess Margaret marries Anthony Armstrong-Jones (later Earl of Snowdon).

1961 Another grandson for the Queen Mother when Princess Margaret gives birth to Viscount Linley.

1966 The Queen Mother goes into hospital for a colostomy.

1969 She attends her grandson Prince Charles's investiture as Prince of Wales at Caernarvon.

1972	After the death of the Duke of Windsor, the Queen Mother meets the Duchess after an interval of many years.
1976	Princess Margaret and Lord Snowdon decide to separate.
1977	The Queen's Silver Jubilee.
1978	Princess Anne's son, Peter Phillips, becomes the Queen Mother's first great-grandchild.
1980	Service of Thanksgiving at St Paul's Cathedral as part of the celebrations to mark the Queen Mother's eightieth birthday.
1981	Prince Charles marries Lady Diana Spencer, granddaughter of the Queen Mother's great friend, Lady Fermoy.
1982	A second great-grandson for the Queen Mother with the birth of Prince William, second in line to the throne.
1986	Prince Andrew marries Sarah Ferguson, who, like the Queen Mother 63 years before, becomes Duchess of York.
1990	Nationwide tributes to the Queen Mother during the golden summer in which she celebrates her ninetieth birthday.
1992	The *Annus Horribilis* of the Windsor Castle fire, the publication of Andrew Morton's *Diana: Her True Story* and the separation of the Prince and Princess of Wales.
1995	Difficulty in walking leads to the Queen Mother's first hip operation.
1996	Divorce of the Duke and Duchess of York, and of the Prince and Princess of Wales.
1997	Diana, Princess of Wales, is killed in a car crash in Paris. At the Queen's Golden Wedding service the Queen Mother walks the length of Westminster Abbey.
1998	After falling at Sandringham, the Queen Mother has a second hip operation and within days is able to take her first steps.
2000	The Queen Mother's 100th birthday celebrations go off in style.
2001	The Queen Mother celebrates her 101st birthday in London, followed by a holiday at the Castle of Mey.
2002	The Queen Mother attends the funeral of Princess Margaret in St George's Chapel, Windsor

Introduction

The door of history closed long ago on the world into which Elizabeth Bowes Lyon was born. But for those who grew old with the century, as she did, that world was not some veiled abstraction. It remained part of them through a lifetime of change such as no generation had experienced before.

When Elizabeth was born on 4 August 1900, the motor car was a novelty, and powered flight still three years away. The telephone was regarded with nervous fascination, even by the few who possessed one. It would be more than two decades before Britain had a system of radio broadcasting, and any thought of television, space travel or computers was still in the realms of fantasy.

In adolescence, and then again in the prime of life, the age group which included Elizabeth Bowes Lyon experienced the two most terrible wars in history. Countless families, the Bowes Lyons among them, lost sons and brothers.

Yet how admirably that generation of 1900 took the twentieth century's convulsions in its stride. The little Victorian, starting life in the age of the hansom cab, and the Queen Mother, stepping blithely in and out of helicopters ninety-odd years later, were one and the same person. No wonder the comedian Arthur Askey brought the house down at a performance to mark her eightieth birthday when he told the audience that he too had been born in 1900, then

The Earl and Countess of Strathmore and their children at St Paul's Walden Bury, Hertfordshire. David and Elizabeth, or the 'two Benjamins', the youngest members of the family, are side by side in the centre of the picture. On the far left is Fergus, who was killed during the First World War.

looked up at the Royal Box and said: 'It was a pretty good year.'

In contrast to the homage that was to come, one can't imagine any great clamour when Elizabeth Bowes Lyon was born. She was after all the ninth child, and even the fondest parent will have got over the high drama by then. But her parents were undoubtedly fond, and her childhood was cushioned by contentment such as anyone might envy.

The Earl and Countess of Strathmore provide a splendid counterblast to the idea of Victorian family life as always loveless and oppressive. As aristocrats – Lady Strathmore was the great-granddaughter of the 3rd Duke of Portland, twice prime minister – they were indifferent to middle-class notions of what was proper. One could guess from his daughter Elizabeth's love of company that the Earl was no unbending paterfamilias. And when she came to Glamis with the Duke of York on their honeymoon in 1923, Lord Strathmore drew a charming Cupid and bow next to their entry in the visitors' book, surely the act of a relaxed and affectionate father.

The Lyons of Glamis come of spirited stock – the blood and thunder of their early history is testament to that. The first was Sir John, granted the thaneage of Glamis in 1372. Four years later he married the King of Scotland's daughter, creating a link between his family and the royal bloodline of the Stewarts which was to be reinforced five and a half centuries later when Elizabeth Bowes Lyon married the Duke of York. Sir John was murdered in his bed, inaugurating a family saga of considerable excitement; though Glamis had quietened down by the eighteenth century when the 9th Earl married Mary Bowes from County Durham.

It is probably not fanciful to read into the Queen Mother's enjoyment of moving from house to house an echo of her childhood. After the death of her husband King George VI in 1952, her life settled into a pattern of stately peregrinations between Clarence House, Royal Lodge (Windsor), Birkhall (near Balmoral), the Castle of Mey, Sandringham, and whichever great house in France she was visiting that year. When you add to that her many official tours abroad, the picture that emerges is of a life spent almost constantly on the move.

In the interview with him which follows, the Duke of Grafton recalled his grandmother, a friend of the Strathmores, telling him of the similiar state of mobilisation insisted on by the Earl. He owned four large houses – Glamis Castle, Streatlam Castle in County Durham, St Paul's Walden Bury in Hertfordshire, and a mansion in St James's Square, London – and he liked to move from one to the other at

Elizabeth Bowes Lyon and her father, the Earl of Strathmore, who passed on to his daughter an ardent love of Scotland.

Lady Elizabeth with her mother, Lady Strathmore, who had an aristocratic indifference to dress, wide-ranging country and artistic interests, and was excellent company. She was the dominant influence on Elizabeth's early life.

short notice with an enormous retinue of servants. Perhaps with his daughter the notice was not so short, and the retinue not so vast, but both loved the stimulus of a change of scene.

It must have taken a very remarkable woman to cope with such an itinerary at the same time as bearing ten children, but by all accounts Lady Strathmore had qualities quite out of the ordinary. One of her eccentricities, her daughter-in-law Lady Bowes Lyon remembered, was an indifference to what she was wearing. It was likely to be the same whether

Glamis Castle (*left*). The family quarters, built onto the side of the medieval fortress, have a contrasting homeliness and human scale. Elizabeth and her younger brother David responded to the romantic surroundings with games of make-believe (*below*). In the one Elizabeth liked best of all, she took the part of a princess.

she was attending to the livestock, or on her way to Buckingham Palace. (The Queen Mother, according to Lady Hambleden, her longest-serving lady-in-waiting, shared Lady Strathmore's lack of interest in that department. Certainly, once she'd decided on a style that suited her, she showed no desire to experiment.)

Lady Strathmore was also amusing, and loved flowers, animals and music, all qualities which in later pages friends attribute to the Queen Mother. Lady Bowes Lyon's story of her mother-in-law's sang-froid when rainwater was pouring down the drawing-room walls is perhaps another clue to the workings of heredity. The Queen Mother was later noted for her ability to rise above the petty turbulences of life. For the Duke of Grafton, who met Lady Strathmore in his youth, it was quite clear that she was the dominant influence on her youngest daughter.

It might be thought that the infant Elizabeth, who evidently possessed the power to enchant from an early age, would have been a spoilt child. But as Lord Home pointed out, with eight older brothers and sisters (though one sister died at thirteen), there was little chance of that. And despite several establishments, or perhaps because of them, the Strathmores were not spectacularly well-off. Handing down shoes from elder to younger was not unknown in Elizabeth's early years, said Lady Bowes Lyon, whose husband David, as last in the family, had every reason to remember.

Elizabeth and David were inseparable. Lady Strathmore, biblically inspired, called them 'my two Benjamins'. During their childhood certain aristocratic conventions, which had barely changed for a century or more, had their Indian summer. With high income, low taxes and cheap labour, sections of the nobility could still live in the truly grand manner which was to become virtually impossible a decade or so later. In this last act of a vanishing way of life the little Bowes Lyons had the run of two contrasting family houses.

Glamis Castle, Shakespeare's setting for Macbeth, is a great medieval fortress at the foot of the Grampians, where in the early 1900s a degree of benevolent feudalism no doubt survived. But Sir Fitzroy Maclean, a Scottish aristocrat a few years younger than the Queen Mother, emphasised during our conversation that the Highlands of those days had fewer of the social barriers which were so constraining in England. He ascribed her fabled capacity for making others feel easy in her company to the early experience of mixing with Scottish children from all walks of life.

By the time David and Elizabeth Bowes Lyon were growing up, Glamis Castle had become a comfortable stately home, though much of the old stronghold is barely changed to this day. It is now doubted that Duncan was really murdered there, but easy to see why the legend was good enough for Shakespeare. There is no doubt about the link between the Lyons and the monarchy, and Charles I hangs among the family portraits to prove it. The happiness of her summers at Glamis, and the sense of blood ties stretching back into history, gave the Queen Mother the passion for Scotland which so stirs that country's expatriates. Unlike most of them, she was able to have the best of both worlds by becoming a resident as well.

In complete contrast St Paul's Walden Bury was firmly in the Home Counties, that cradle of English class distinction. Though even there, as Lady Bowes Lyon heard from her husband, he and Elizabeth spent much of their time with servants and estate workers, in the tradition of aristocratic children. Encircled by Hertfordshire's gentle undulations, The Bury (as it is known in the village) is a roomy Queen Anne country house, whose colony of barns and outbuildings was the perfect bolt hole when the youngest Bowes Lyons wanted to get away from their elders – siblings as well as parents. 'Don't tell May, she'll tell Mother,' was the standard cry – May being the eldest sister.

By 1915 Lady Elizabeth was contributing to the war effort as both nurse and occasional stall-holder for charity.

It is easy to see how such an upbringing bred in the Queen Mother that attachment to a country style of life, which so many of those who knew her commented on. 'She walks the hills like few people one has seen,' was the way Lord Home described it. Taking the dogs out was a daily ritual whenever she was at Royal Lodge or in Scotland. She told the Duchess of Grafton she missed her dogs more than anything else when she was abroad. And Ashe Windham's interview has a graphic description of her wrapped up against a howling gale, with the corgis trotting along behind. Lord Charteris, though, had one proviso: 'She's a countrywoman, but I don't think she'd be happy without London.'

The seeds of London pleasures were sown in childhood too. As the Queen Mother later reminisced to Lady Bowes Lyon, a family outing to the pantomime was a performance in itself, starting with a seven-mile drive to Hitchin station during which the children had to walk up the hills to save the horses. For a country girl in 1910, however well-born, a West End theatre must have been seductive indeed – a riot of gilt and crimson plush, where the gods of entertainment worked their magic. Her trips to the pantomime fired Elizabeth Bowes Lyon with a delight in show business which never left her.

The idyll came to an end on the opening day of the First World War, Elizabeth's fourteenth birthday. Rarely can an anniversary have marked the end of childhood with such finality. Within a year the growing-up process had been accelerated by the shock of bereavement; one of her brothers, Fergus, was killed on the Western Front. Glamis Castle, no longer alive with the sounds of a large and cheerful family, became a hospital for wounded soldiers and Elizabeth was immured there with her mother for the duration of the war. In many ways it must have been a sobering adolescence.

But, as the testimony of her friends indicates later, not the least of the Queen Mother's remarkable qualities was her resolve to make the very best of the prevailing circumstances. That cheerful tendency was already there in the fifteen-year-old Elizabeth; and far from lamenting at the unfairness of a war which had cut short her pleasures, she took on the role of deputy to her mother at Glamis with success. There are letters to prove it, for not only did she help to run the castle, but she also put her heart and soul into bringing comfort to the wounded. She soothed them and entertained them, and simply by exercising the devastating charm that came naturally to her, made them forget their troubles. According to General Watson of the Black Watch, the letters they wrote to her in later years show her to have been an 'angel' in the improvised wards at Glamis. Already, long before the mantle of royalty added to the enchantment, that extraordinary gift for making people feel that they mattered to her was in evidence.

Meanwhile a rather sketchy education was being completed by governesses. It became even sketchier towards the end of the war when her mother was ill and Elizabeth virtually ran the castle. But Lady Strathmore was a cultivated woman, and to say that her youngest daughter was under-educated would be a distortion. She learnt good French and the ability to write simple but heartfelt English prose, which later made recipients of her letters, like Mrs Peter Cazalet, glow with remembered pleasure. Examples of her rounded, widely spaced handwriting, thanking people or, in the case of the old servant mentioned by Canon Treadgold, commiserating over a death in the family, are no doubt treasured in homes all over the country.

A letter not by her, but about her, in the Grafton family archives, sheds a fascinating sidelight on the conduct of the upper classes during the First World War. They sacrificed their sons unstintingly, but some things they would not give up. So, well before the end of the war, the seventeen-year-old Lady Elizabeth Bowes Lyon 'came out'. Lady Strathmore gave a dance for her, and in the letter quoted by the Duke of Grafton, his great-grandmother wrote percipiently of the 'hearts Elizabeth will break'. In another letter, a month later, the verdict was that she was by far the most charming of all the debutantes. There was nothing so vulgar then as a Deb of the Year, but had there been, she would surely have carried off the honours. 'Not a classic beauty, but charm that could take the bird off the tree – and always fun,' said Lord Charteris, who was thirteen years her junior, but whose stepfather knew her at the time.

As the soldiers, or some of them, came back from the trenches, there was an understandable urge to make up for time stolen by war, and among the young swells Elizabeth

Many young aristocrats coming back from the war fell for the boundless charm of Lady Elizabeth Bowes Lyon.

Bowes Lyon was all-conquering. 'I should think they were absolutely dotty about her,' said Lord Charteris. 'She swept the board,' a contemporary later told Lady Longford. 'She had endless admirers,' remembered Lady Hambleden, who first met her at her own coming-out ball in the early twenties.

Among them was a painfully shy young man with a nervous stutter, who in 1920 had been made Duke of York by his father King George V. It says a great deal for the Duke's tenacity of purpose that he allowed neither his own handicaps, nor the lady's lack of encouragement, to deflect him from his goal. In the end it was sheer dogged determination that won her, but not before she had had serious misgivings.

In those days newspapers were more restrained in discussing the love lives of the Royal Family, but among those in the know, its lack of progress was much talked of. According to Lord Hailsham, his father, who was Attorney-General at the time, told him over breakfast one morning that Lady Elizabeth was 'hesitant' about accepting the Duke of York.

There are any number of possible explanations. Lord Hailsham senior believed she was afraid of the role she would have to play, even though at that stage there was no reason to suppose that she would ever be queen. Lady Hambleden, too, felt that she delayed in order to think through the momentous implications of marrying into the Royal Family. According to Lady Longford, who discussed it with the Queen Mother's contemporaries while writing her biography, it was because she had been denied a normal youth during the war, and wanted time to enjoy her freedom.

Whatever her doubts, they were finally swept aside by her suitor's resolve. From Glamis to St Paul's Walden Bury he pressed his claim, and in January 1923 was rewarded with acceptance. The recollections of Mrs Lilian Thrussell, then the young daughter of an estate worker at The Bury, give a charming picture of collective intuition working overtime in the village, when the Duke of York and Lady Elizabeth most unusually failed to turn up at church one Sunday morning. The suspicion that an engagement was in the offing was borne out by events, and there was much rejoicing in Hertfordshire and far beyond. 'They seemed made for each other,' was Mrs Thrussell's verdict, and the nation felt likewise. Queen Mary thought that Elizabeth was 'the one girl who could make Bertie happy.'

The marriage of the Duke and Duchess of York three months later was the making of the gauche young bridegroom. It also blew a healthy gust of fresh air through the somewhat stuffy environs of the Court, described by Lady Jean Rankin as 'very buttoned-up and not at all relaxed'. An observant young footman, Charles Oulton, later to rise high in royal domestic service, found the Duchess 'very different from the sort of people we had seen before – European princesses and so on'. Mr Oulton shared the general view that George V liked his daughter-in-law enormously, and there was rarely any doubt about whether George V liked someone or not. He even relaxed his ferocious attention to time-keeping, and made excuses for her when she was late for dinner.

One can see how the arrival at Court of this unaffected young woman, with the 'ordinariness' Charles Oulton noted, began the process by which the monarchy was to adapt and develop over her lifetime. Of course, no one of such magnetism, apparent long before she became royal, can be ordinary, but one knows what Charles Oulton meant. Her naturalness and the warmth of her responses were qualities which George V and Queen Mary, for all their virtues, couldn't muster.

Of course another member of the Court was pushing more impatiently at the frontiers of change – the Duke of Windsor. But in contrast to his sister-in-law, the heir to the throne was to prove a futile reformer. Far from relaxing his

(*Above*) Lady Elizabeth Bowes Lyon leaving her London home in 1923, on her way to marry the Duke of York, second son of George V. After a long courtship she had finally accepted him, to the delight of both families, and of the nation at large. They spent part of their honeymoon in Surrey (*right*) before moving north to Glamis.

George V and Queen Mary (left) were devoted to their daughter-in-law, the Duchess of York. The arrival of the Yorks' first child, Princess Elizabeth (fifteen months old when this picture was taken), gave the Royal Family a new focus of popular interest. The Duchess's parents are on the right.

father's inflexibilities, he incurred his disapproval, and the undoubted influence he had with the public was destined to vanish down the cul-de-sac history had waiting for him.

But history had not yet shown its hand, and the young Duchess of York settled effortlessly into the role she had every reason to think would be hers for life. In the 1920s the pressures of royal status were not what they have become

In spring 1936 the Duke and Duchess of York and their daughters seemed the very model of family contentment. But upheaval was only months away.

for her descendants. The glare of publicity was less unremitting and the habit of deference rigorously instilled. Her upbringing was patrician and she was used to the burdens of eminence, albeit not on the scale encountered by royalty.

Women of that generation did not question the principle that it was their task to support their husbands and propagate the species. Two attractive daughters soon enhanced the standing of the Duke and Duchess of York in the eyes of the public, and fatherhood brought to the Duke a contentment he had not known before. But the slowly emerging growth in the confidence of this shy man owed much to her extraordinary devotion.

In one of those curious episodes in which paths cross, and then recross to dramatic effect, a young pupil at Haileybury, Peter Townsend, was in the front row when the Duke and Duchess of York visited the school. Looking back with the perspective of someone who later knew them well, Townsend remembered the difficulty the Duke had in getting out his words, and the 'waves of sympathy' which the Duchess seemed to communicate to him. Several of the recollections which follow stress her incalculable influence on his capacity for the task ahead.

Edward VIII's abdication in 1936, in order to marry the divorced Mrs Simpson, was without doubt the pivotal moment in the life of the woman who was to become Queen. One has only to imagine the outcome if it hadn't happened. Assuming for the sake of argument that Edward had been persuaded of the error of his ways, had abandoned Mrs Simpson, had married and had heirs, then the position of the Duchess of York would have been unchanged. Stretching before her would have been a lifetime of motherhood, good works and benign obscurity of the sort enjoyed by her sister-in-law, the Duchess of Gloucester – though the radiance of her personality would still have imposed itself on the public consciousness.

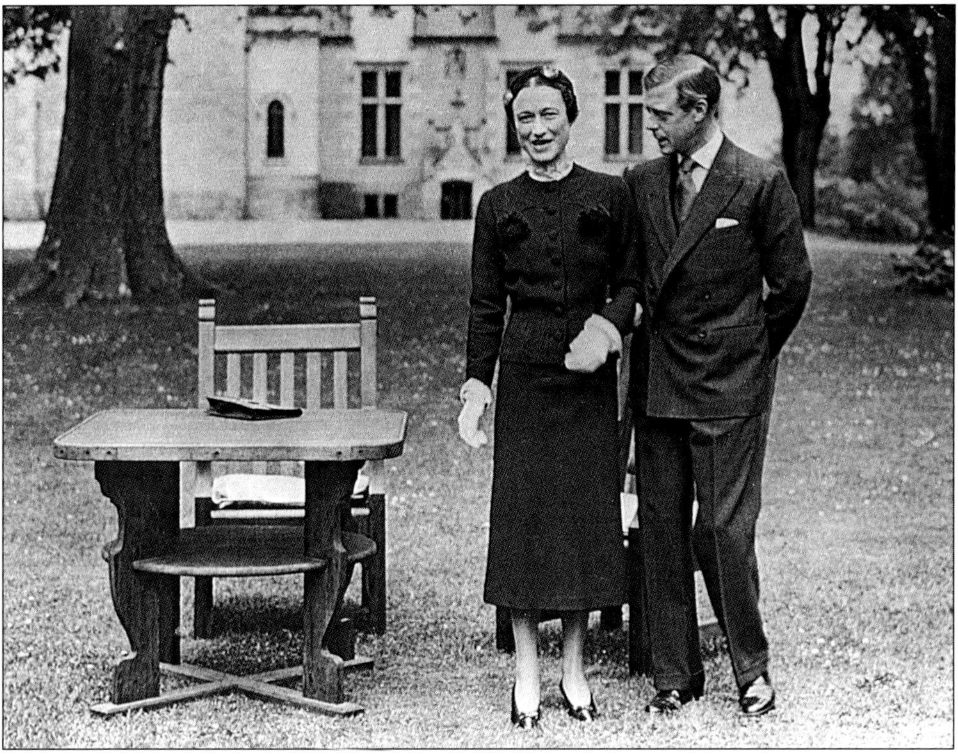

(*Above*) The Duke of Windsor in France with Mrs Simpson, five months after the Abdication. A month later they were married.

The Queen Mother greeting the Duke and Duchess of Windsor in London in 1967. She had not met the Duchess for thirty-one years.

Whether that is the way she would have preferred things to go, perhaps even she could not be sure. There is an almost universal feeling, which she must have been aware of, that as far as the country was concerned it turned out emphatically for the best. 'I often think that Mrs Simpson ought to be thanked, rather than reviled,' was the way Lady Jean Rankin put it. But the new Queen believed then that the burden of kingship placed on her husband was one for which he was not equipped, and believed later that his manful acceptance of it 'shortened his life', as Lady Jean recalled. Her alleged resentment of Mrs Simpson, for setting out to ensnare Edward when her divorced status ruled out any possibility of her becoming queen, was often cited as a stain on the Queen Mother's reputation.

Looked at another way, it proved that she was human. Was it any surprise that she, who saw more intimately than anyone the strain the Abdication placed on her husband, should harbour not altogether friendly feelings towards the woman she felt had precipitated the crisis? After Edward and Mrs Simpson became Duke and Duchess of Windsor and went abroad, it was evidently Queen Elizabeth, rather than the King, who refused to countenance suggestions that the Windsors might in due course come home. When they did return briefly on the outbreak of war, only the King met the Duke, and neither he nor the Queen received the Duchess.

In later life the Queen Mother's natural humanity caused her to relax whatever antipathy she felt, and she twice met the Duchess of Windsor with no sign of ill-will. By this time, according to her close friend the Duke of Grafton, she was loath to talk about the Abdication. He tried to get her to write her own account of it, but doubted that she would (if he was wrong, what treasures lie in store for some future royal historian). The Duke insisted that, in his discussions with her on the subject, the Queen Mother was extremely

A hint of the King's misgivings can be seen in his expression on Coronation Day in 1937. In contrast, Queen Elizabeth seems undaunted by the task ahead.

generous about the Windsors. 'She really hadn't got a clue what she was dealing with,' was apparently the worst the Queen Mother had to say of the Duchess. And, 'You don't know how we loved him,' was her epitaph on the Duke.

But in 1936, with the monarchy in worse trouble than it had been for 250 years, she can surely be forgiven for resenting the way that she and the King had been 'landed with it' – the phrase she used when talking to the Duke of Grafton. Despite George V's stated misgivings about his eldest son's suitability for the Throne, no one had thought to educate the Duke of York, his brother's heir presumptive, in the rudiments of kingship. He was obliged to learn them as he went along. Nor was the new King's health robust, and his stammer, though improved, meant that public speaking was agony for him. Not surprisingly he felt inadequate to the task.

Fortunately his Consort did not feel inadequate to hers. With her uncomplicated patriotism, love for her husband, and belief in the institution of monarchy, the support she gave him in sustaining the Crown can hardly be overestimated. It's easy to misjudge from a distance the danger to the constitution as it appeared at the time; but a popular figure had been unceremoniously banished, and his awkward and little-known brother put in his place. Would the system survive such an upheaveal? Or would the country turn against the usurper of its favourite? 'It was a time of turmoil, and the sense of values of the British people was upset,' was how Lord Home, then an MP of five years standing, remembered it. 'It might have gone very wrong,' was Lord Carrington's assessment. 'It was not good news. The Royal Family was given a nasty knock,' said Lord Charteris.

All were agreed that Queen Elizabeth's part in seeing the crisis through was crucial. 'Her good humour and poise steadied things,' said Lord Home. Speaking at the time, the Earl of Derby, politician and diplomat, went further. According to the Duke of Grafton, who heard it from the Earl's grandson, he declared: 'That is the lady who saved the monarchy.' The explanation of how she did so lies in the recesses of her character, but two very contrasting witnesses used the same thought to describe an aura they were aware of in her presence. Mrs Lilian Thrussell, the estate worker's daughter, saw it as 'the most marvellous, calming, lovely atmosphere'. While Sir Peter Ustinov noted that 'an extraordinary pool of calmness seems to spread around her'. If ever a calming influence was needed it was at the time of the Abdication.

To emphasise the qualities Queen Elizabeth brought to

It was felt by many that Queen Elizabeth's calming influence made the period following the Abdication less troubled than it would otherwise have been. Here she and the King are visiting new council flats in Shoreditch, London.

bear during the emergency is not to belittle the King. Whatever his private trepidation, he faced his responsibilities with a constancy and courage which slowly turned popular feeling in his favour. But those in a position to know maintain that he could not have managed without her. In the view of Lord Charteris, her part in the drama was 'very important constitutionally'. Lord Hailsham felt that no one could have done it better.

The woman who was not to become Queen Mother for another fifteen years soon came to be seen as the embodiment

'The family on the Throne.' The King and Queen brought a flavour of domesticity to the monarchy with which households throughout the country could identify.

of both queenliness and motherhood. After the decent severity of George V and Queen Mary, and the raffish and ill-fated bachelordom of Edward, the arrival of a King with a wife people could warm to, and two bewitching little daughters, turned out to be the tonic the monarchy needed. 'They picked it up and put it right where it is – the family on the Throne,' said Lord Charteris. Indeed the way the institution developed over the next half century clearly had its origins in the beau ideal of family life, which Queen Elizabeth established. 'The perfect consort' is how she was described in more than one interview. She also managed the delicate fusion of the roles of both wife and subject of the King. Whatever the extent of his reliance on her, she always deferred to him in public. 'If I asked her if she would do something,' her lady-in-waiting Lady Hambleden recalled, 'she'd always say: "I'll just ask the King".'

After the Coronation in 1937, they had only two years of peace in which to consolidate the renewed stability of the Crown. It was their success in doing so which was later to have such a bearing on the way the country faced up to Nazi Germany. As Lord Hailsham put it: 'The monarchy operated by that married couple was a very important factor in keeping public opinion united and firm, and determined to go on, when on paper we'd lost the war in 1940.' But before that, as peace ran out in the summer of 1939, a triumphant tour of North America had repercussions which were no less momentous.

Charles Oulton, the Palace servant who accompanied the King and Queen, was struck by the enormous crowds who turned out to cheer them across Canada and into the United States. At Washington station they were met by the President and Mrs Roosevelt amid scenes of pro-British fervour. 'That really was an occasion,' said Mr Oulton, though expectations had been quite different. Transatlantic sensitivities about the snooty British had led to a belief that it was plain

(*Overleaf*) The King and Queen visited America in 1939 amid scenes of pro-British fervour. Queen Elizabeth is in the front car with Mrs Roosevelt.

TREASURY
PLACE

anti-Americanism, rather than her two divorces, which lay behind the rejection of Mrs Simpson.

Well ahead of the rest of the world in their tolerance of divorce, but still with the touchiness of a young nation, some Americans were prepared to take offence. That they didn't probably had more to do with sentimental notions of kingship, not unknown in republics, than with the still somewhat wooden figure of the King. But Queen Elizabeth's gift for seeming to be approachable, while at the same time occupying a plane that was out of bounds to ordinary mortals, was so similar to the spell cast by Hollywood film stars that the Americans loved her. She came across the footlights in a way that they, as the inventors of show business, understood. And besides, she was related to George Washington via ancestors with the intensely democratic name of Smith.

Relations between countries are many-sided, and their protean course can be hard to chart exactly. But the reinforcement of Anglo-American goodwill deriving from that tour was to have some part, at least, in determining the future foreign policy of the USA, and thus in the outcome of the Second World War. The President and Mrs Roosevelt had liked the King and Queen, and so had their fellow-Americans. A year later, with Britain standing alone against the Nazis, the ties of friendship established just before the war allowed Roosevelt to coax his country away from isolationism. The Lend-Lease agreement of 1940, bringing American arms and money to Britain in her hour of need, was crucial to the ultimate defeat of Hitler. The King and Queen deserve some of the credit for that historic chain of circumstances.

When war was declared on 3 September 1939 the Queen was a month past her thirty-ninth birthday; Princess Elizabeth was thirteen and Princess Margaret nine. Had things been different she would have been looking forward to the onset of early middle-age with her usual equanimity. The next six years must have tested even her composure, yet the pool of calm she seemed to inhabit throughout life showed scarcely a ripple.

Probably the greatest service the King and Queen performed during the war was simply in being there. At a time of great peril 'they symbolised the continuity of family life', said Lord Hailsham. 'Though at the top of the social tree, they remained what ordinary families are.' When it was suggested that her daughters might be evacuated to a safer country, the Queen's reply had a defiant ring about it: 'The King couldn't go. I couldn't leave the King. And the children couldn't leave without me.'

The Princesses were sent for safety to Windsor Castle. The King and Queen divided their time between Windsor and Buckingham Palace, which was the target of no fewer than nine air raids. One, in which they were nearly killed when a bomb fell in the inner courtyard, is referred to later by Peter Townsend – the former pupil at Haileybury who had shown such interest in them on the day they toured his school as Duke and Duchess of York. He was by now a war hero with the DSO, DFC and Bar, and they were about to make their second appearance in his life. After valiant service in the RAF, in 1944 Group Captain Townsend became equerry to the King, an appointment which was to have dramatic consequences nine years later. But at that stage the chief preoccupation was the danger to life and limb. Among Townsend's recollections is of the time he was having coffee with the King and Queen after dinner, 'and there was the most enormous explosion. Everyone rose about a foot in the air.' Sent by the King to investigate, Townsend discovered that a V2 flying bomb had fallen on a pub not far away, killing hundreds of people.

It was the experience of being in the thick of it herself that led Queen Elizabeth to make her celebrated remark: 'I'm glad we've been bombed. It makes me feel I can look

(*Above*) The King and Queen inspecting the damage caused by one of nine bombing raids on Buckingham Palace.

(*Left*) Queen Elizabeth talking to ARP (Air Raid Precautions) wardens after a raid in London.

(*Top right*) The King and Queen visiting homeless people in Sheffield in 1941.

(*Right*) Queen Elizabeth in rural Berkshire with the land girls in 1941.

The balcony of Buckingham Palace on VE day in 1945. Amid the smiles of rejoicing the King's face shows signs of strain.

the East End in the face.' There have been murmurings that it was absurd to compare the suffering in the East End with that of people in Buckingham Palace, but Lady Longford's reply is to the point: 'It is just the same to die in a palace as it is in a tenement.'

When dwellings of whatever sort were destroyed in the bombing, the King and Queen saw it as their duty to visit the bereaved and homeless. There is plenty of contemporary evidence that the journeys of George VI and Queen Elizabeth to the stricken cities of Britain were welcomed as demonstrations of true concern.

In the early part of the war the Duke of Grafton was a young subaltern at Windsor and saw a good deal of the Royal Family. His view of the intimate family circle shows how differently the King and Queen responded to the stresses of those visits. 'The King was highly strung and, I think, exhausted by them. But there she was, bright as a button after the most harrowing day, always amusing, making jokes, larking around until midnight, and then off again the next morning.' As her Private Secretary, Sir Martin Gilliat, was to say of her many years later: 'She has a great ability not to worry unnecessarily. What must be, must be.' That simple but sustaining philosophy saw her through the vicissitudes of life with the minimum of wear and tear.

When the war ended in 1945 the King and Queen shared the sense of deliverance felt by all survivors. As they embarked on what were to be their last few years together, the return to a settled family life brought them a period of intense happiness they had not known since the carefree days before the Abdication. As a parent, Queen Elizabeth held the reins lightly, though according to Group Captain Townsend, 'there was an invisible discipline'. Lady Hambleden remembered her as 'a very good mother. She would never reprimand her daughters in public, but would tick them off afterwards.'

The Queen's instinctive lightness of touch set the tone for their family life. Charles Oulton, their servant for many years, recalled the pleasing domesticity of her time at the Palace, in contrast with its function as a royal workplace in later years. A picture of jolly family evenings, conjured by Queen Elizabeth out of nothing more than a sense of fun and a pack of cards, emerges through the memories of Group Captain Townsend. 'We had the most tremendous laughs – maybe doing a little post-mortem after a big "do". They liked to see the comic side of life.'

Because of her sweet smile and exquisite public decorum,

Queen Elizabeth the Queen Mother's character could have been interpreted as somewhat sugary. The vignettes of those who knew her well show that nothing could have been further from the truth. The secret of her perennial freshness through so many decades of public life lay in her ability to get a little amusement out of the people she came across. 'A lunch in one Town Hall is very similar to lunch in any other Town Hall,' was the dry observation of Major Tom Harvey, her Private Secretary after the war, 'though you never get the slightest hint of *déjà vu*.' The reason was that she found people not only interesting, but funny. She was 'excellent at talking to statesmen and politicians', Lord Charteris remembered. 'And perhaps later laughing at some of them a bit too – getting fun out it.' The humour could be very much to the point. According to Sir Fitzroy Maclean, 'It was kindly meant when kindliness was deserved; not quite so kindly when it wasn't.' The Duke of Grafton spoke of her gifts as a comedienne. 'She was terribly observant and a brilliant mimic. She'd notice some mannerism one hadn't noticed oneself, and be very, very funny about it afterwards.'

George VI was noted for the occasional explosion of bad temper, when the stammer he had conquered would briefly return. Queen Elizabeth used humour to mollify him, and it would soon be forgotten. 'If he got cross, she would always, in a clever way, turn the whole thing round and it became a joke,' said Lady Hambleden. The Duke of Grafton noticed how she was 'forever soothing him, and if he was rather nervous, she only had to arrive in the room and the whole atmosphere would change.'

The King's health had always been delicate, and in 1947 it was clear that the strain of his duties was beginning to tell. He and the Queen, taking Princess Elizabeth and Princess Margaret with them, set off early that year on a gruelling tour of South Africa. 'I only hope we survive,' was Princess Elizabeth's reaction on seeing the itinerary. Her remark

Eleven years after the Coronation, the King and Queen celebrate their Silver Wedding anniversary in 1948 with a service in St Paul's Cathedral.

carried overtones of foreboding for the King of which none of them was aware. He survived, but lost well over a stone in weight as the hectic three-month tour ground on, and was never quite the same man again.

But on their return such anxieties gave way to parental rejoicing over Princess Elizabeth's engagement. Because of the war, opportunities for a show of royal pageantry had been almost non-existent since the Coronation ten years before. So when the heir to the throne married the Duke of Edinburgh in Westminster Abbey a month before Christmas, the pomp rivalled any that had gone before. As a virtuoso of the small but winning detail. Queen Elizabeth arranged

A moment's peace for the King and Queen from their relentless schedule.

for a sprig of white heather from Balmoral to rest beside every place at the wedding breakfast table.

With her older daughter married, and Princess Margaret at seventeen beginning to build a life of her own, the Queen took her usual sanguine view of changing circumstances. 'They grow up and leave us, and we must make the best of it,' she said. Among the compensations in 1948 were the silver wedding of the King and Queen, and the birth of their first grandchild, Prince Charles. But the King's health was deteriorating. Arteriosclerosis was causing him pain in both legs, and despite an operation early in 1949 he never fully recovered. The most conscientious of monarchs, he was depressed by the economic plight of the country and by the Korean war. He had an operation for lung cancer in 1951, but early the following year, a few weeks after his fifty-sixth birthday, he died of a thrombosis.

Throughout the King's last illness Queen Elizabeth had kept the worst from him, and remained, at any rate on the surface, her characteristic buoyant self. But according to Lady Longford, 'when she came back from Scotland towards the end, the strain was so great that for the first time she slipped into a side entrance at Buckingham Palace without seeing the public.' And with the King's death even her unflinching spirit was crushed, and she gave way to inconsolable grief.

Though she could be said to have been the stronger character of the two, Queen Elizabeth was too feminine, and too much of a traditionalist, not to have relied heavily on her husband. She had always known his worth, and despite qualities that had seemed unpromising for kingship, with her help he had grown in wisdom and stature. For his subjects the death of George VI was simply the passing of a well-loved Head of State, but for his widow it was incomparably more.

Her desolation was such that for a long time, said Lady

(*Left*) The King and Queen bidding farewell to Princess Elizabeth as she leaves for a tour of the Commonwealth in 1952. The King had less than a week to live. (*Above*) Three Queens mourn the passing of George VI.

Bowes Lyon, 'there was nothing anyone could do'. In the autumn when she went to Birkhall, near Balmoral, she was still refusing to see anyone. But staying at the castle as a guest of the new Queen was the Prime Minister, Winston Churchill, and at the suggestion of Lady Jean Rankin he arrived at Birkhall one day unannounced. Lady Jean, who had been a lady-in-waiting since 1947, believed it was Churchill's persuasive powers which 'made her realise how important it was for her to carry on'.

The Queen Mother outside the Castle of Mey which she bought in 1953. Her northern retreat in Caithness helped her to come to terms with the loss of the King.

Still grieving, and not yet settled into her new role as Queen Mother, she travelled to the far north-east corner of Scotland to stay with friends. It was this visit which more than anything brought meaning and purpose back into her life. Caithness was part of the land of her forbears, but unlike Glamis and Balmoral it was unfamiliar. As the pain of bereavement slowly eased, the attractions of a place with no shared memories was strong, and in the far-off flatlands she found one.

Lady Jean Rankin was with her the first time she set eyes on the Castle of Mey. 'When the owner told her he was going to take the roof off, she said: "oh no, you can't do that, it's much too beautiful",' Lady Jean recalled. Having decided she would like to save the castle from ruin, she secured it 'for a trivial sum'. Lord Thurso, with a castle of his own just along the coast, felt she was looking for much more than accommodation with character. 'I think what also appealed to her was that it needed somebody. She thought that if she loved it, it would love her back – and indeed it has.' To see house purchase in such human terms may seem fanciful, but the love affair with Mey endured for the rest of her life.

The Queen Mother moved out of Buckingham Palace and into Clarence House just before the Coronation in 1953. With her went not only Princess Margaret, but also Group Captain Peter Townsend, the former equerry to the King, now Comptroller of the Queen Mother's Household. The love that had grown between her daughter and the recently divorced Townsend confronted the Queen Mother with her second crisis in just over a year. The first had deprived her of a husband. In the second, it was the lack of one which allowed the situation to get out of hand.

A central ingredient in the Queen Mother's make-up was the ability to 'rise above difficulties', as her old friend Lady Jean Rankin put it. For someone whose bad times may have been no worse than many other people's, but who had to live them out in public, it was an enormous asset. One way of rising above difficulties is to pretend they are not happening, and it's reasonable to ask how a mother, who was said to be acutely observant in other contexts, failed to notice that her daughter was falling in love with a divorced member of her own staff. 'If the King had been there, it would never have reached the climax that it did,' believed Lady Longford, a view shared by a close friend of Princess Margaret's at the time.

The clue to the Queen Mother's singular oversight may lie in one of the contradictions in her character. For an inveterate traveller she was extraordinarily addicted to permanence. She hated her staff to retire – in her old age even elderly maids were kept on simply because they had been with her for so long. Group Captain Townsend had worked for the Royal Family since 1944, and she valued the associations kept alive by his continued presence in her Household. The fact that the King had liked him so much was comforting. Lady Longford, who knew Townsend in those days, saw 'what a charmer he was', and it is really no surprise that Princess Margaret thought so too. The death of her father, to whom she was very close, had left a vacuum in her life. It was filled by the handsome war hero of thirty-seven.

Did the Queen Mother, still distracted with grief, not realise what was happening? Or, with her gift for rising above difficulties, did she prefer not to realise? Whatever the answer, any hopes she may have had that the problem would solve itself if she ignored it, were to be disappointed. Outside Westminster Abbey on Coronation Day reporters noticed Princess Margaret laughing with Group Captain Townsend as she dusted a speck from his uniform. Within a fortnight the story of their romance was out.

Applying the rigid standards of the day, Church and Court made clear that, for someone so close to the throne, marriage

Group Captain Peter Townsend (back) had been the King's equerry. When the Queen Mother took him onto her staff, he and Princess Margaret fell in love.

to a divorced man was out of the question. Princess Margaret could have gone ahead, but only by giving up her royal status. So in the end orthodoxy prevailed, and she and Townsend parted. Looking back, many years later, he spoke warmly of the Queen Mother: 'She was extremely concerned and worried. How could she be otherwise? But she was simply wonderful all the way through.' Once things had reached the state they had, her strength and ready sympathy were invaluable, though it may have been her failure to act sooner which caused them to arise in the first place. It was inherent in the Queen Mother's unrepining nature that she should have wanted to keep up with Townsend afterwards. She invited him to her eightieth birthday party, and on another occasion, after they hadn't met for years, she caught sight of him and gave a little sign 'that one used to make when dancing the Boogie-woogie'.

As the tribulations of the early fifties passed into history, the Queen Mother embarked on her long reign as a national matriarch. With subtlety and tact she never over-shadowed her daughter the Queen, and seemed to occupy a separate realm of her own, with a broad-brimmed hat as a crown, and robes of powder-blue chiffon. The Queen, with equal tact, deferred to her mother over small details. One of them, according to Canon Treadgold, concerned the forms of service at the Royal Chapel in Windsor Great Park. For although it is the Queen's private chapel, it adjoins Royal Lodge, and the Queen Mother's religious inclinations were always respected. That they were strictly traditional is hardly a surprise – in general the only changes she liked were ones of scene. At the first service he took in the Royal Chapel, Canon Treadgold read the passage about Solomon and Sheba from the 1952 Revised Standard Version of the Bible. 'What a lovely story that is, Chaplain,' the Queen Mother said to him afterwards, 'and in my version such lovely words.' He took the point and went back to the King James Bible of 1611.

Once she had made up her mind to something, the Queen Mother was not to be deflected. Two of her long-serving courtiers used the same word to describe her exceptional tenacity. 'She has a core of steel inside her,' said Sir Alastair Aird. According to Lady Jean Rankin: 'She has a gentle exterior, but great strength underneath it. Steel.' Imposing her will through sound and fury was not the Queen Mother's

By her sixtieth birthday the Queen Mother had three grandchildren, and had settled comfortably into the role she was to play for decades to come.

style – Sir Alastair and Lady Jean both testified to her even temper. Rather it was a question of the telling glance. Those who worked for her soon learned to read the signals. 'She would keep the smile going, sometimes with a little difficulty,' said Peter Townsend, 'but the eyes would gleam, and that was enough,' Sir Alastair remarked on her 'steely blue eyes', and described how 'if you put a foot wrong, you will know it.'

Away from the Household, strong men yielded before the combination of feminine charm and fixity of purpose. Getting her own way, Lord Annan recalled, was a matter of 'lifting her eyebrows slightly and giving you a quizzical look, as if to say: "I wonder if you could do that." And you knew you ought to do it.' Once, while she was Chancellor of London University and he was Vice-Chancellor, Lord Annan stood firm against her wish for things to stay exactly as they were, and finally won her reluctant support for a planned innovation. He proposed to sell off the university press, which offended her on the grounds of family loyalty as well as general resistance to change. The press had been named after her predecessor as Chancellor, the Earl of Athlone, who was Queen Mary's brother – quite enough to make her disapprove of the sale.

Sir Peter Ustinov, her guest on a number of occasions, sensed that she was far too alert to the way things were to let her natural conservatism take over completely. 'She is redolent of all the niceties of another age, yet disregards them really.' Sir Alastair Aird, a member of her Household from 1960, remembered how the ritual of putting a suit on for tea in the country eventually gave way to shirt-sleeve order, under pressure from her grandchildren. Sir Martin Gilliat and Lady Hambleden, who knew the Queen Mother as well as anyone outside her family, both testified to her belief in fixed standards of behaviour. She was of the opinion that too many of them had 'fallen by the wayside', but what saved her from anything remotely resembling censoriousness was her sense of humour. She saw the funny side far too readily for that.

The Queen Mother's taste in comedy was of the music-hall kind enjoyed by much of the population. 'She loved the Crazy Gang. They were pretty lavatorial, and that goes, provided it's funny as well,' was Sir Martin Gilliat's assessment. Sir Peter Ustinov observed how heartily she laughed when there was 'a low comedian around', and for Frankie Howerd, her favourite in later years, she was 'a performer's dream. She goes there wanting to laugh.' On television she liked the *Two Ronnies* and *'Allo 'Allo*, and when Lady Longford had inadvertently held up proceedings at a dinner party the Queen Mother was attending, she said: 'Don't apologise. It's marvellous – I've been able to watch *Dad's Army* through from start to finish.'

She also liked to put on a comic turn of her own – Lady Jean Rankin remembered her surprising her guests after dinner with a creditable impersonation of Charlie Chaplin. And the guests themselves discovered that a readiness to sing for their suppers was often the governing factor in whether or not they were asked again. 'She likes outgoing people,' said Sir Martin Gilliat. Ministers of the Crown and ambassadors were expected to gather round the piano after dinner and perform. The material could be 'Come Into The Garden, Maud', still in the piano stool at Sandringham from Edward VII's time, old music-hall numbers like 'My Old Man Said Follow The Van', or the songs of Noël Coward, preferably with the composer at the keyboard. We have Lord Carrington's word for it that Lord Hailsham's tuneless rendering of the *Marseillaise* became an annual fixture at Royal Lodge. And the sight of cabinet ministers, tagging along behind the Queen Mother in a conga all over the house, was fondly recalled by Lord Charteris from visits to Balmoral.

(*Above and right*) A determination to get as much out of life as possible was the Queen Mother's guiding principle. Whether fishing in New Zealand in 1966, or, much later, exploring Venice for the first time, she went on embracing new experiences into late old age.

At eighty-five the Queen Mother showed few signs of taking things easier. In this birthday portrait she was joined by the Prince of Wales, Prince Edward, Princess Anne and Prince Andrew.

(*Right*) Family and entertainment – two much-loved elements in the Queen Mother's life came together when she joined Princess Anne and the Princess of Wales at the première of *A Passage to India* in 1985.

As a hostess she was in the rarefied position of being able to ignore many of the social changes of her lifetime. Her lunch and dinner parties would not have shamed the grandest Edwardian household, with footmen in attendance and, as Lord Annan remembered, 'course after course of good, sound, hearty English fare'. General Watson spoke of 'the table absolutely groaning with silver and fruit and china'. And her neighbour in Caithness, Lord Thurso, described a picnic by the river as 'the most magnificent alfresco meal' he had ever had in his life, with hot food, and all the guests at tables and chairs. The remoteness of the Castle of Mey protected that kind of expedition from prying eyes. There,

By a twist of fate, the Queen Mother will be remembered as an owner more for one horse that lost, than for her multitude of winners.

Elizabeth Bowes Lyon, aged two, in her high-chair.

Elizabeth, aged seven.

Elizabeth in 1907, looking every inch the Earl's daughter.

(*Above*) Lady Elizabeth Bowes Lyon, aged 22.

(*Opposite*) On the threshold of marriage in 1923.

(*Above*) The Duchess of York with the young princesses at Royal Lodge, Windsor, in 1936.

(*Above*) The Queen with her daughters at Windsor Castle in 1941.

(*Left*) The King and Queen at Buckingham Palace.

(*Previous page*) As Queen in 1941. Outward serenity at the height of war.

she was not so much Queen Mother as respected local cattle-breeder.

A lifelong taste for being surrounded by people, combined with the means to indulge it, accounted for the sheer scale of the hospitality. According to Mrs Ewen, her housekeeper at Birkhall, the Queen Mother liked the house 'bursting at the seams'. Yet her vitality never flagged. 'We in the Household are amazed that she never appears to want to have a jolly good yawn,' remarked Sir Martin Gilliat, who attributed her stamina to the fact that she was 'not a fusspot at all'. It made her an uncomplaining guest as well, whether in a freezing French chateau, as the Duchess of Grafton recalled, or at interminable public functions. Her ladies-in-waiting marvelled at her willingness to stand for hours making conversation to strangers with no sign of boredom or fatigue, and Lord Home remembered how, after just such a day, she was ready to dance till two in the morning. His theory was that she must have had 'very good digestion'. Her belief in doctors, according to Sir Martin, was 'slightly tenuous', and she expected others to rise above illness, just as she did.

This sound constitution made the Queen Mother impervious to the weather, and many are the comments from friends about her refusal to let wind and rain stop her doing what she had come to do – an invaluable asset in her chosen sport of steeplechasing, where an English winter often contrives the foulest conditions. For all her success as an owner, it was a spectacular failure which guaranteed her racing immortality. In the 1956 Grand National her horse Devon Loch, ridden by the man who was to become her favourite thriller writer, Dick Francis, inexplicably belly-flopped within sight of a great victory. 'That's racing,' was the way the imperturbable owner commiserated with her jockey.

If the Queen Mother was ever ruffled, no one would have guessed. Once when her helicopter was forced down with engine failure, her equerry Ashe Windham recalled, she

On her ninetieth birthday the Queen Mother was still 'putting on the best show she could'. Close observers rated the performance 'absolutely genuine'.

calmly waited for a replacement and climbed back on board. Sir Peter Ustinov's account of how she dealt with a barrage of toilet rolls at Dundee University is less hair-raising, but an indication of her steadiness under fire. She merely handed the missiles back to the students, whose attempt at *lèse-majesté* collapsed forthwith.

But these were pinpricks; the royal convulsions of her final years were a different matter. The divorce of the heir to the throne was not something to be brushed aside as one of life's little predicaments. And yet she had 'risen above' the divorce of her own daughter at a time when such a thing was far more shocking than in the 1990s. Now that same buoyant unconcern came to her rescue again, as marital breakdown became the dominant royal theme of the decade. Of course she was aristocratic rather than royal, coming from an upper-class which continued to take infidelity and scandal in its stride during the long years of royal respectability. And so, distressed as she must have been when her grandchildren's marriages failed and Diana met a terrible death, she did not let it cloud her life. Her health faltered in her nineties, but after hip and cataract operations it visibly improved and she sailed serenely on, her popularity growing ever greater as that of her family declined.

Naturally there was an unreality about her public persona. But it was unreal not because of what was there on display, but because of what was hidden from view. Millions of admirers never had the chance to hear her slip into dialect to take off a pompous official she'd met that day, or give vent to those strong convictions over which Sir Fitzroy Maclean and other friends felt they must 'draw a definite veil'. (They consisted of no more than the standard prejudices of ladies of her generation and upbringing.) And to that extent the public appearances were only a small part of the story. The writer Lord David Cecil, who knew her from childhood, once called her 'a performer', meaning someone who wanted to put on 'the best show she could.' While quite aware of the theatricality involved, her audiences sensed that the side of her they did see was not phoney, but was simply one aspect of the whole person. 'A great performance, but an absolutely genuine one,' said Lord Charteris. She was gracious and considerate and interested. But she was a human being, not a paragon, which meant she was also sharp-eyed, funny at other people's expense, and liked her own way.

From time to time sections of the intelligentsia, anxious to be thought immune to her spell-binding ways, found fault with this or that aspect of the Queen Mother's character. She could afford to ignore them. As one of the monarchy's more memorable consorts she is guaranteed the esteem of future generations long after her critics have been forgotten. Even in her lifetime she was too popular for them to attract much attention, and now she is gone, her niche in history is secure. In every place she adorned with her presence, from the shores of the Pentland Firth to the far corners of the world, she will live in the remembrance of people, and the affection they felt for her. Nowhere was this demonstrated better than at the extensive celebrations for the Queen Mother's 100th birthday. After receiving a telegram from her daughter, signed 'Lilibet', the Queen Mother rode from Clarence House to Buckingham Palace through the cheering crowds, in an open carriage adorned in her favourite racing colours. Her busy day continued with an appearance on the Buckingham Palace balcony and a family lunch, topped off by a visit to the Royal Opera House to watch the Kirov Ballet. As the country celebrated, the Queen Mother could be left in no doubt about her continuing popularity.

JAMES HOGG

Long life, strong character, and the workings of history have made the Queen Mother the most enduring public figure of the twentieth century. Her place in the national pantheon is secure.

At a reception in Salisbury
the Queen Mother made new friends
and greeted old acquaintances
as she did wherever she went
throughout her life.

Friends, Relations and Acquaintances

Gregarious by nature, and a public figure since 1923, the Queen Mother had a vast circle of friends, and a phenomenal memory for names, faces and incidents from the past.

Lady Bowes Lyon

Widow of the Queen Mother's youngest brother, David. She remained a close friend long after he, by then Sir David, died in 1961, and she continued to live at St Paul's Walden Bury, the Bowes Lyon family house in Hertfordshire.

It was 1929 when I first met her, when she was Duchess of York. She was very much the same person then as now – same fun and sense of humour, imagination, and self discipline, which somehow releases her to make fun in any situation. She was always close to David – there were only a couple of years between them – and until the end of his life they were just as close, in spite of having both married.

When they were children at St Paul's Walden Bury they had all sorts of hiding places. Queen Elizabeth was here the other day and she said it brought back so many happy memories of where she and David used to play. There was Charles May's workshop with fascinating objects in it. Then there was the Bell House, with a very deep well, a chaff-cutting machine and a stone grinder. When I first came to live here the workshops really looked as if somebody had hung up their coat and gone away for dinner and not come back for twenty years. There was still a coat hanging up and hammers and tools all laid out.

Whenever they were up to something it was always: 'Don't tell May, she'll tell Mother.' May was the eldest of the ten children and they were the youngest. They were much loved but I don't think spoiled, because if you have older brothers and sisters they take good care you aren't spoilt.

I remember hearing from my eldest sister-in-law how she had a suitor of whom Elizabeth and David disapproved, and how they took it in turns to walk up and down the drawing room

Lady Bowes Lyon gives her sister-in-law a tour of the grounds at St Paul's Walden Bury.

when he was trying to propose to put him off. It worked. Then, when they were eight and six, they went to a tea shop with somebody who, as their Mother explained, wasn't very well-off, so they shouldn't order the best cakes. So when she asked them what they would like, David said: 'We will have whatever is the cheapest!'

There was always an annual visit to the pantomime, and this involved taking all the children seven miles to the station. They had to walk up the hill to save the horses. They saw George Robey and Nelly Wallace and all the stars of the day. When they got back to King's Cross invariably most of them were sick with the excitement and food. It was something they relived and enjoyed for the next six months.

In the early days, before their father inherited Glamis, they weren't very well-off. It was really a case of handing down shoes from elder to younger. They certainly couldn't maintain the garden as it is now. Lady Strathmore – Lady Glamis as she was then – had awfully good ideas about how a formal garden ought to be laid out, but never quite enough cash to carry it out! Things that ought to have been flat ended up on a slope. At one stage she embarked on keeping polo ponies for which she got no support from the family. So that came to grief, although she had some very good ponies. She was a woman of wide interests, and culture and she was a talented musician. I think that's where all the family got a sense of good taste and a love of plants and animals. It was certainly handed down to her younger ones.

Another story about Lord and Lady Strathmore is when they were driving through Hyde Park. Lady Strathmore had a cold, so she had to sit by the chauffeur on the box in the front of the car, because Lord Strathmore didn't want to get it. He was sitting in the rear of the car, which had stopped at a traffic block at Hyde Park Corner, when who should draw up but Queen Mary in her car. And there was the lovely Lady Strathmore sitting in the front of the car, probably in the same clothes as she'd been feeding the chickens in that morning.

There's a nice story about the time it was decided to put another bathroom in the Bury. Charles May, who was the sort of general factotum, said everything was much too expensive and he could do it far cheaper. So the family went away, as usual when things were done in the house. When they came back, however, they didn't find another bathroom, but a second bath put in the same bathroom. That was much cheaper! So a partition was put up, but there was no ventilation for the second one and you could only go in if you fanned the door to get the steam out. It's now been converted to a linen cupboard, much more suitably.

When I came here we had to do so much to the house. There were electric wires popping in and out of the woodwork and only two bathrooms in the whole house. I remember sitting on a sofa with David's mother during a thunderstorm, and I looked up and saw that the red silk on the walls was pouring wet. I said to her: 'Look what's happened.' And she said: 'Good gracious! We must move the sofa out,' and that's all we did. So when we came to live here there were mushrooms sprouting and dry rot everywhere.

It was a very happy childhood for Elizabeth and David and whenever they met over the years it was entirely natural – they just picked up where they left off. When I think of her it's her sense of fun I remember, but also her self-discipline, which is very strong. When there are troubles her discipline masters her emotions, such as when my husband died. She was a great strength to me then. I saw a lot of her, and I was so grateful that the friendship continued when there were just the two of us. She'd been through it herself; you could cut with a knife her desolation when the King died. There was nothing that anybody could do, and it took years for her to take an interest and enjoy anything, but she eventually overcame that. But she does feel things very deeply – even when her detective died some years ago. She said: 'I've seen more of the back of that man's head for eleven years than I've seen of any of my family'. He went up the hill at Birkhall just for an afternoon's climb and was found dead, and that was a terrible shock for her. She is a very compassionate person.

The Dowager Countess of Strathmore

Widow of the Queen Mother's nephew, the 17th Earl. The Queen Mother was her guest at Glamis Castle on many occasions.

The very first time I saw her was long before I knew my husband, when I was lucky enough to be presented to the King at Buckingham Palace when I was eighteen. I had no real contact with her, so I suppose it wasn't until I was engaged to my husband that I met her properly. She couldn't have been more wonderful and more welcoming to me, and she gave me a lovely family ring for a wedding present, which I shall treasure all my life. I think everybody, to a degree, feels they know her well. I hadn't known her personally until then, but when I did it was an extension of what I think I'd always felt about her. It has been the most wonderful relationship ever since.

She was an incredible help to my husband and me when we inherited Glamis and we had to get it back into a happy family home again, after some sad years of disrepair. She was a wonderful strength and support, and encouraged me and did everything she could to help us with suggestions. She was really so very appreciative of what we were doing, which I find immensely heart-warming.

When she comes here it is lovely to hear what Glamis used to be like in the old days and her memories of a very happy childhood. I think one of the loveliest memories that she often speaks of is when she was a child, galloping on her pony up the drive on frosty mornings with the air whipping against her cheeks, and galloping down again coming home for breakfast. That is a very happy memory of hers. I also remember her telling me something that she thinks is her very first memory. She recalls as a very small girl – I think she must have been about four – sitting on her grandfather's knee, looking out at the fairylights in the trees and the fireworks that were celebrating her grandparents' golden wedding. That was 1904, because I think her grandfather must have died very shortly after that.

Apparently the Queen Mother and her brother David kept a pig in the round turret on the lawn. One day the great-uncle of the man who told me this story was mowing the lawn, when out of this turret burst a pig being ridden by the Queen Mother as a very small girl, chased desperately by her brother David. The two of them must have had a wonderful time together, being so much younger than the rest of the family. The Queen Mother herself told me a story about her brother David. He hated the little yew trees that had been planted the other side of the Castle, so one day he pinched some poison from the gardeners, and when the grown-ups were all having dinner he climbed out of bed and went out and poured the poison all over these trees. All was discovered and I should think he was given a frightful rocket for it, but the trees grew better than ever. The Queen Mother sometimes looks at them when she stays here and says: 'Look at David's trees, they're doing all right.'

The Queen Mother spent most of the 1914–1918 war up here, when Glamis became a convalescent hospital for a great many soldiers. She was fourteen when it began and eighteen when it finished. I think she completed her education here with a governess, but she also helped to look after all the soldiers and did a tremendous amount. In fact, towards the end of the war when her mother wasn't well, I think she pretty well ran the whole of Glamis, and did a wonderful job. It was much appreciated because soldiers used to come back, who'd been here in the war. Later when she was with the King on tours, in Australia in particular, because there were a lot of Australian and New Zealand soldiers here, she'd be in some official line-up and suddenly she'd catch sight of a face that she knew in the crowd and she'd rush off and say: 'Hello Tom, Dick or Harry, wonderful to see you again,' and it would be somebody that she'd known here, and they'd be so pleased to see each other.

She has a fantastic memory. When I've shown her old photographs she would immediately say who was in the background. For instance, somebody in the village gave me a photograph of her and the King arriving at Glamis station when they were newly married. I showed it to her and she immediately said: 'Oh yes, that's Mrs McGuiness the gardener's wife behind, and the stationmaster's name was ...,' whatever it was – I've forgotten already, but she remembered everybody's name from way back.

She tries to come here two or three times a year. One very definite occasion is every autumn when she visits the Lord Roberts

The Dowager Countess of Strathmore in the Queen Mother's sitting room at Glamis Castle.

Workshops in Dundee, which she's done for well over fifty years. She always either comes to lunch here first and we go to Dundee together, or she comes to stay the night before. It is wonderful but there is never enough time to see everything, and to ask all the things I want to ask her about – time seems to fly past. It is a most heart-warming occasion, because of the way she enhances everybody's lives. She never fails to go into the kitchen and see everybody who cooks the lunch for us. And when she leaves everyone feels marvellous and is smiling from ear to ear, happy because they have been able to do something for her.

There aren't so many people here now that remember her when she was young. There was the widow of the old, retired head forester who, when I first knew her, always talked about 'Lady Elizabeth' because she'd known her as a child. I also knew a wonderful person called Miss Fox who'd been one of the first Girl Guides when she started the pack in Glamis. She's dead now, but she used to help us here. Miss Fox would wait in the dining room for us to come in for lunch and Queen Elizabeth would go forward to say, 'Hello Miss Fox, how lovely to see you.' Miss Fox would do her beautiful curtsey; the pleasure on both sides was so apparent it was lovely to see. Queen Elizabeth is so pleased to see the people she knows again; she feels she is coming home, and everybody treats her just as she's always been treated at Glamis.

I've asked myself just what are the qualities that endear her to people, and I think she is the person who enhances everybody's lives more than anyone I know. But as well as all the obvious things we know about her, I think underneath there is a tremendous strength and courage that perhaps sometimes people don't know. She is the sort of person if you were in trouble you could say anything to and she would give you the wisest possible advice. She is also such a happy person. When you are with her the flowers seem to smell better, the sun shines more – even when it isn't out! She is interested in everything and everybody. It is remarkable that with all that her life involves, she is still interested in me, in my family, all our problems, all our joys and all our sorrows. It isn't just that she is trying to be nice or say the right thing. It really matters to her. It is terribly important to her that everything at Glamis goes right and is done as it has always been. She was greatly, greatly overjoyed when my grandson arrived, and she knew there was another generation coming along to be at Glamis.

The other thing I feel about her is that even if she hadn't married the Duke of York and become Queen, she would still have been equally wonderful. I think the great blessing that was given to us all was that she did become Queen and that more people had this wonderful feeling of happiness that spread from her, not just her own family and circle of friends.

When she comes to stay she always sleeps in the same room, the one Princess Margaret was born in. That's an event that's well-remembered even now at Glamis. The best memories of it were from Miss Fox who remembered it distinctly. It was a very hot August day. So hot that when she bicycled back from Forfar all the tarmac was melting on the road, and her bicycle kept getting stuck. In the evening there was a crashing thunderstorm just at the time that Princess Margaret was born. The next night they had a tremendous bonfire out on Hunter's Hill. The mother of the girl who lit the bonfire is still alive, and the girl, who's now a married woman. So I've been lucky enough to hear memories of that too.

I just can't imagine life without her. But I think, in a way, we shall never be without her – the strength, the example, the happiness and the way to approach life and people, that we've all learnt from her, will go on through many generations. She has certainly been the most important influence on the whole of my life.

The Duke of Grafton

His family connections with the Queen Mother's family go back to Victorian times, when his great-grandmother was a near neighbour of the Queen Mother's grandmother, Mrs Scott, at Roehampton. The Duke often travelled abroad with the Queen Mother.

My great-grandmother, Mrs Hugh Smith, and my grandmother, Lady Buxton, were both absolutely devoted to Queen Elizabeth's mother, Lady Strathmore, who was obviously a remarkable person and, I should think, a very formative influence in her life. I've always had Cecilia Strathmore held up to me as a sort of model for her perfect family life. I remember years ago my grandmother trying to describe to me the atmosphere with the ten children, though it became nine because one girl died, aged thirteen I think. It made a great impression on me. I think that Queen Elizabeth has the same effect. She produces this extraordinary atmosphere of tranquillity and calmness and wisdom and humour.

Her mother, Cecilia Strathmore, didn't have a very easy life because Lord Strathmore was rather eccentric and used to say suddenly that he wanted to move. And they moved with a huge retinue of servants from Glamis to Streatlam in County Durham, a huge and beautiful Charles II house which was destroyed after the last war. Then to St James's Square in London, where they had a beautiful house by Robert Adam, or to St Paul's Walden in Hertfordshire. So they had four houses to revolve around. It must have been rather hard work, if you had nine children and an enormous household to move.

I remember being taken by my grandmother in 1937, the year of the Coronation, to another house, in Bruton Street, to be introduced to Lady Strathmore. I was only about eighteen. She

The Duke of Grafton.

was small, dressed in black and obviously very amusing. I don't know why I should remember it, but she showed my grandmother with pride two little chocolate figures of the King and Queen which she'd bought that morning and stuck on the mantelpiece. They'd obviously given her great amusement. I think Queen Elizabeth was absolutely devoted to her. The whole family were. They were very fond of their father as well, but Lady Strathmore was obviously a remarkable person and I think she was probably stronger than her husband. I am certain that some of Queen Elizabeth's extraordinary characteristics descend directly from her mother.

Unfortunately I parted with some rather interesting letters my great-grandmother wrote while staying at Glamis in about 1908, in which Queen Elizabeth was mentioned as a very pretty child and charming to look at. They had daily prayers in the chapel at

Glamis, and apparently everybody wore lace caps and she sat beside her mother in the front pew. There are two more letters written by my great-grandmother to her daughter in 1918, referring to the then Lady Elizabeth Bowes Lyon. The first says: 'Elizabeth Lyon is out now and Cecilia has had a dance for her. How many hearts Elizabeth will break.' That was 11 March 1918. The second, a month later, says: 'It amuses me very much hearing of the different debutantes. Sybil (Lady Bicester) says that Elizabeth Lyon is by far the most charming of them all.' So that obviously shows that she was an extraordinary person at eighteen.

I think her arrival on the scene in the early twenties when she became engaged to the Duke of York was a wonderful breath of fresh air. She was never frightened of King George V – she was very fond of him, and she must have been a great help in a slightly, perhaps, sticky atmosphere. She made jokes and she made everything fun, which I think they had never really known before. She became very fond of George V and always says: 'Wasn't it lucky I wasn't frightened of him?' She was also very fond of Queen Mary, with whom she used to do trips all over the country. They went to Sandringham and Balmoral and were quite undaunted by distance; they did miles in those huge Daimlers. I have begged her to write down her earliest reminiscences, which are rather fascinating.

She was brought down to Sandringham to be introduced when King George V and Queen Mary and six children were all stuffed into York Cottage, which was a horrible house on the edge of the garden, while Queen Alexandra was living with her sister, the Dowager Empress of Russia, in the big house. Queen Elizabeth was very keen to be introduced, and described these very old people looking critically at her; both deaf, and very foreign, but nice and friendly. All that is linked with history. The Empress had guarding her the Cossack guard she had brought out of Russia with her. There is a portrait of him at Sandringham.

I didn't meet Queen Elizabeth until the winter of 1940 when I left Sandhurst and joined the training battalion of the Grenadier Guards at Windsor. It was a terrible time just after the Battle of Britain and immediately before the really bad bombing. There were very real fears that the Germans might land and kidnap the

Princesses, who were never allowed out of the Castle grounds. A company from the training battalion was posted in the Castle and five officers slept in the Castle, and the mews was turned into barracks for the guardsmen. The harness room was the orderly room, and two of us had to have all our meals with the Royal Family, which is really how I got to know them so well. There were the two Princesses, two governesses, and various members of the Court. But what remains absolutely imprinted on my mind is the terrible time the Queen and King were having, because they were going off to visit bombed cities every day. I should think the good she did was absolutely incalculable but very wearing. They left the castle at eight in the morning and they used to get back at eight in the evening. Then they had their dinner alone in a room in the corner of the castle. The castle was like a morgue; all the pictures were facing the wall and all the furniture had been taken away. The staff had their dinner next door and at about ten o'clock the King and Queen used to join them. And there she was bright as a button after the most harrowing day, where she had exhausted herself exuding sympathy. But she was always amusing, making jokes and larking around until midnight, and then she was off again the next morning. It was a most extraordinary experience. The King was highly strung and, I think, exhausted by it, and she absolutely kept the whole thing going in my view. She made a deep impression on me and I was only twenty-one. You can't possibly exaggerate her importance. Also, of course, at the time of the Abdication. A friend of mine called Richard Stanley was the grandson of old Lord Derby, the former ambassador in Paris. I remember once in the very early days, Richard saying to me: 'My grandfather says that is the lady who saved the monarchy.' Coming from Lord Derby that was quite something.

Queen Elizabeth has never liked talking about the Abdication, but if one can get her to talk about it she says things of extreme interest and importance. I long for her to write something down, but I am sure she never will. However, I would like to refute these horrible books which people keep producing, inventing that she had a feud with the Duchess of Windsor and that sort of thing. She has never said anything nasty about the Duchess of

Windsor, except to say she really hadn't got a clue what she was dealing with, which I think is an understatement. As for the Duke of Windsor, she would say: 'You don't know how we loved him.' Describing the Abdication all she said was: 'And then he went.' That is also an understatement, particularly as I understand the Duke and Duchess of York were never consulted. She used to say they were absolutely landed with it, but that there was no alternative. And they weren't sure how people would react. Edward VIII had this extraordinary position in the country, and she used to say: 'We didn't know whether the country would accept us.'

It is very difficult to describe exactly how she was such a source of strength to the King, but she was forever soothing him, and smoothing the path, and dealing with difficult people. If he was nervous, she somehow only had to arrive in the room and the whole atmosphere would change. She is extremely clever and has got this genius with people. I remember her once saying: 'Don't you think dealing with people is the really important thing,' and my goodness, she really knows how to do it. When she comes into a room it is like sunshine. I remember once at Sandringham, many years ago, she had had flu and her absense was very much felt. She suddenly appeared, walking down the stairs, and you felt the whole atmosphere change at once, although she still wasn't feeling very well. She is also terribly observant. You don't realise it but she notices everything in the nicest way and can be very funny afterwards about it. She notices somebody one perhaps hasn't noticed oneself at all, some mannerism or something. She is an actress, a really brilliant mimic, and she can imitate them exactly. Always in a kindly way, but frightfully funny.

It was after the war that our friendship really grew. My wife and I were lucky enough to be asked to Windsor very soon after we were married, during that tragically short time that they had after 1945. They really had had the most awful time – the Abdication, followed almost immediately by the war, and then there was very little time for them to enjoy themselves before the King's health failed. We used to see them regularly. We were staying at Sandringham a fortnight before the King's death and he seemed perfectly all right. Queen Elizabeth is an optimist and she thought it was going to be all right. She didn't really face what was happening. In a way it was merciful it happened as quickly as it did. As usual she was gallant, but absolutely heart-broken. Somehow, though, she rose again and faced the future.

One forgets that she was still quite young, and there was no particular role for her to play. What she did was to make a unique role for herself, and I think largely because of the extraordinary width of her interests – there is nothing she is not interested in, from racing to poetry. She has these delightful weekend parties every spring – usually arranged by Ruth Fermoy, her lady-in-waiting – of poetry readings and music, with Peggy Ashcroft reciting. Every July we stay at Sandringham for the King's Lynn Festival, which she has supported for over thirty-five years, and which has marvellous music. She talks to a jockey or to a leading musician in exactly the same way, and they all feel that they are the one really important person in her life. That is a very great gift.

We also had the good luck to go on many expeditions abroad with her, where all these qualities come out. Our trips to France started in 1964 – the first one was to the Loire. She was a friend of Sir Piers Dixon, who was then ambassador, and she had said to him: 'Oh, I would love to go to France; I don't know France at all well.' And he said: 'Why don't you come?' I think she took a floor of a hotel near Tours and we saw the chateaux of the Loire and all that area. In the years that followed we went all over France, staying mainly with private people, which was again very interesting because she was hurled into completely strange surroundings. She didn't know the people or the place, and they were all rather scared. They thought: 'The Queen Mother is coming to stay, we must be on our best behaviour.' Of course, in a trice they were all eating out of her hands and she luckily speaks very good French.

Later we used to go to Italy, to Venice and to Tuscany, and we did a lovely trip to Sicily and Naples on the *Britannia* which I think she thoroughly enjoyed. She loves sightseeing, and is quite undaunted by heat and cold. She doesn't notice matters like that and nor are you supposed to. I think perhaps the most interesting place we have been to is her grandmother's villa outside Florence – this was Mrs Scott, her mother's mother. She said she would so much like to see the house which she remembered as a child. I was rather nervous because we didn't know the people who were living there and it might not have been well looked after, which would have upset her. Not at all, they were a very nice young Italian couple who had just bought it and were looking after it beautifully. She walked in from the street and straight into the hall and said: 'Oh yes, I often remember Granny sitting in that chair.' Then she walked out into the garden where there was this wonderful view of Florence, and she said: 'I think I can remember Granny laying out this garden.' It was very unfortunate they didn't really understand English, so I don't think they understood quite how historic it was. It was seventy-five years earlier that she'd been there with her Granny and her brother David in the Easter holidays, and she had not been back to Florence since.

If I had to name an outstanding quality I think it would be her courage. She is undaunted. It isn't that she doesn't feel things deeply – she does – but she seems unquenchable. I think that whatever horror has happened to her she has somehow surmounted it because she has deep faith, which is very important in situations like that. I think she accepts it as a vital part of life. She has also been sustained by her passionate patriotism, and her sense of duty. Whatever happens she will go on doing her duty till she drops. I've never met anybody who really criticised her in any way. Since I've known her over fifty years, that is absolutely remarkable. She is an outstanding person and I can't think that we, as a country, have really deserved such a bonus. It was a marvellous bit of luck.

The Duchess of Grafton

Mistress of the Robes to the Queen from 1967, she and the Duke were invariable travelling companions of the Queen Mother on private visits abroad.

I met her just after we married. We went to stay at Windsor for Ascot and we were lucky enough to see her very frequently after that. The main thing about her is what fun she is. Immediately she walks in the room everybody cheers up. We also have had quite a lot of time on our own with her, walking in the woods at Balmoral, and on a lot of journeys. She is always interested in one's own life and she remembers everything – things you've told her many years before – which is a marvellous quality, especially when you consider the number of people that she knows well. She has the gift of making close friends with people, though not as close as family. I think the Queen rings her up almost every day, and I know that when the Queen is away on tours her mother misses her very much indeed. I think she worries just a little. The tours are very arduous and she has often told me how thankful she will be when the Queen gets back.

She is a great traveller herself, and some of the tours we have been on with her, supposedly private, can be very arduous. Some were amazing because they had perhaps been arranged by her friend Jean-Louis Lucinge and she didn't even know the people she was going to stay with, so there was great excitement arriving. We used to see the people on the airstrip, waiting for us, very anxious, and we would look out of the aeroplane and say: 'Good heavens is that the Duke?' But within half an hour she had made friends with them. Then we would drive to their chateau or whatever it was. The next event was to see her bedroom, because everybody prepared a wonderful room. Once she had to steer her way between plants which had been brought in from the garden.

The Duchess of Grafton.

We have stayed with a wide variety of people on these visits, many of which were to France. Sometimes it is perishingly cold and she has just one little fire in the bedroom, even when the snow is falling. Not that she is bothered about the cold. She is just as happy going out in pouring rain as in good weather. The meals on these trips can go on for a very long time, and there is an immense amount to eat, which is a slight worry. But she enjoys the whole thing. She always gets to know the people on either side of her, all about their family, and finds out the most extraordinary things that have happened to them. She usually has a prefect or a mayor beside her, and sometimes they don't speak English, so it is difficult for her. Occasionally, before the meal starts, she would be told by the host, 'So and so is a communist,' and she always said, 'But I love communists,' and would proceed to get on particularly well with them. She is never wearied by it at all. I have never known her to be tired or to sit back. She always sits upright, which is extraordinary for somebody of her age. She has tremendous stamina. I think it is because she enjoys everything she docs. She is always saying, 'Oh what fun!' whatever we have to do. I think she is stimulated by people. Every day is completely full, and she goes to bed very late, which is tiring for some of our older friends. She has marvellous health, is hardly ever ill and never has a headache. She just rises completely above it.

We look back and think how much we have enjoyed everything we have done with her. She's very spontaneous. If we come back on a nice day having had lunch out somewhere she might say: 'Shall we take a thermos?' and we'll set off again for tea, and go up somewhere. Or she might say: 'Would you like to come and just see the sunset at the hill behind?' She always has some new idea and isn't set in her ways at all. She loves the outdoors, and even when we get back from a long day she always sets off, perhaps to take her dogs out – they are great companions to her. I once said, flying back in an aeroplane: 'What did you miss most while we were away?' and she said: 'The dogs.'

The Countess of Longford

As Elizabeth Longford, historian and author of a biography of the Queen Mother.

I found some very interesting glimpses into her childhood when I was writing my biography of her, especially one written by a great friend of her mother, Lady Strathmore, while on a visit to Glamis. This is what she wrote: 'The two little ones, David and Elizabeth, are sweet creatures. Elizabeth lovely; David was an imp who wanted to be revenged on me for something I had innocently repeated to his mother, and stole my telephone and ran away with it all over the castle to Cecilia's despair (Cecilia is Lady Strathmore). Before leaving Glamis I must note the morning service in the chapel, and the lovely group of Cecilia sitting between David and Elizabeth, Cecilia and Elizabeth wearing little caps, for it is the custom of Glamis not to let a woman creature attend the service with her head uncovered.'

She seems to have had a very happy time growing up at St Paul's Walden Bury, dependent a good deal on her brother David. They really could enjoy themselves, and would run away and make a little home of their own with their animals and all their friends. She was very imaginative too; she liked to think the place was haunted by friendly ghosts, and it was full of love of flowers and trees and moss and stones. They made jokes about the grandeur of the place, like the names they gave to the classical statues in the garden – the 'running footman' and the 'bouncing butler'. All in a cheerful, child-like spirit. I think she has the same light-hearted and very sensible attitude to all her homes. She takes them very seriously, but she can be funny about them. For instance, the ghosts of Glamis. She used to show visitors around and as they passed the great-grandfather clock doing its tick-tock, she would point and say: 'There is the ghost.' She loved dressing-up romantically and she certainly, like many little girls, would like to dress up as a princess and say: 'I am Princess Elizabeth.' She was a romantic and Glamis certainly brought out the romanticism in her, but never on a solemn or pompous scale.

She had to be a performer a lot when she grew up and I think that is the key word. In no sense is she artificial or putting on a show of performing. Lord David Cecil, who was a very intimate friend of hers, and had known her as a child, first used this word 'performer', and said that she performed in the sense that she felt it was her duty to put on the best show she could; that the people wanted this and expected it. She always makes the best of every situation and gives it a liveliness which other people wouldn't bother with, or wouldn't be capable of.

Her mother was a tremendous influence, first in her run-of-the-mill education, and a very cultivated, literary one it was – she read them Bible stories and so on. But I think she also gave her, in a very quiet way, her ideals. It wasn't done pompously, but in a way that she remembered. One of the things that her mother said was: 'Never look at your feet.' This has worked in two ways all her life. She has always walked perfectly, knowing she is not going to put a step wrong; and secondly, she is never flat footed, literally – she never wears flat heels. She has gone through life on high heels. She has always had an ideal to look up and walk high. Her mother has been described as old-fashioned, but she was a woman of very high ideals and high culture, and a tremendous influence in the family. The influence really radiated from her.

When she came out as a debutante she had an absolutely smashing impact on society. A friend of mine who was a young man at the same time said to me once: 'Everybody fell in love with her; we were all in love with her.' He said he wanted to marry her, but everybody did. She just swept the board, including the Duke of York, of course. After he proposed to her, she thought it over for a very long time before she accepted him. He wasn't one of the pack; he was somebody she had to consider very seriously. It is quite a puzzle. I personally think the reason was that she was a young girl, who had not had a normal youth because of the war – it was rather overshadowed – and then when she came out she wanted a bit of freedom, and to see the world. She also realised, none better, that if she married a royal prince,

The Countess of Longford.

there would be a great many duties attached and was she going to be able to take on this new life? I think she did think it over very carefully, and she was won over by his utter determination, a characteristic that he always showed; resolve and determination. He was terribly shy and had an awful stammer, and I think she felt convinced he needed her. That is one of the things that has always operated with her all her life – if she was needed, she immediately wanted to give what was necessary. That was one reason she decided to marry him, and it was very fortunate for him and for the country that she did.

The Abdication was a terrible period for her, the most awful strain. It was worse for him, and he had a short nervous breakdown. His official biographer describes him as being numbed with shock, and I think she must have felt almost the same. She had influenza at the time, and I'm sure that was made worse by the situation. In a way she was helpless. But though she was passive as regards the events, she was very active in supporting him. After the Abdication was over, she knew that she was going to be the one who had to support him and help rebuild the monarchy. She was absolutely type-cast for it. It was a most amazing providence that we should have had someone like her at that critical moment.

She was very important during the war too. She was tremendously courageous and determined, and knew that we were going to win. When it was suggested that perhaps her children could be evacuated to a safer country like so many others, she made her famous remark: 'The King couldn't go, I couldn't leave the King, and the children couldn't go without me.' And then that other famous remark when they bombed Buckingham Palace and she said, 'I am glad in a way that we have been bombed; now I can look the East End in the face.' Some people have said that that was absurd, that you could never compare the suffering of the East End with the suffering of people living in the Palace, but if they had been hit, it would have been just the same to die in a Palace as it would have been to die in a tiny little tenement.

It must have been a great strain to her when the King's health began to fail. Thinking of her as a woman, she had to conceal it, up to a point, from him and be always smiling – one can never imagine her without a smile – and support him. I don't think he knew exactly the seriousness up to the last, but we do know that when she came back from Scotland towards the end, the strain was so great that for the first time she slipped into Buckingham Palace without seeing the public. She was terribly devastated when he died, really knocked out for a time. People began to think that perhaps she would retire to the Castle of Mey and do a Queen Victoria, but of course that was never on the cards. It was just a question of time and one or two incidents which were going to bring her back again.

After the King's death his equerry, Group Captain Peter Townsend, became Queen Elizabeth's Comptroller of the Household. He and Princess Margaret fell in love, but were obliged to part because of his previous divorce. I knew Group Captain Townsend when he was young, and so I know what a charmer he was. I can well understand that both the King and the Queen were extremely fond of him, and indeed all the Royal Family were. As a mother with a longing for her daughter to be happy, one can see that it was a very complicated situation. She must have hoped against hope that it would turn out all right in the end. And it would have, but for the divorce. We have to remember that was the key thing in those days. It was a long time ago. I sometimes wonder if that wasn't the time when she most of all wished her husband had still been alive, because I think if he had been there it wouldn't have reached the climax it did. I just can't see Group Captain Townsend going up to King George VI and asking for his daughter's hand.

My own meetings with the Queen Mother made me devoted to her. I always remember being incredibly touched when, after she had that quite serious operation many years ago, and she came back for the first time to a reception in Buckingham Palace, we were all trooping past and I said: 'Ma'am, I am so pleased that you are back with us again,' and she gave the most wonderful look, as though she was really grateful, though why she should be I don't know. She said: 'Thank you so much, it is so good of you to say that,' as though she really felt pleased at being wanted. Then there was an occasion when I was going with my husband to stay with mutual friends, to see some races (incidently it poured with rain the whole weekend, so there wasn't a single race). The rain began on the Friday night, and I was driving. It was pitch dark, I lost my way and we arrived about an hour late. So the dinner was made extremely late, and when we were brought in I felt like crawling and made profound apologies. She said, 'Don't worry at all, don't apologise. It's so marvellous – I have been able to watch *Dad's Army* right through from start to finish.'

I would say that she is one of nature's great pleasure-givers. I remember once when her daughter, the Queen, was on a train which was held up and a lot of people were gathered. And the Queen said: 'If mummy were here she would be out of this train immediately and dashing down and talking to all of these people.'

Mrs Margaret Bruce

Born a few years before the Queen Mother, she was the daughter of the butcher in Kirriemuir, near Glamis. She often met the Queen Mother when they were children.

The first time I was at Glamis Castle would have been in about 1904 or 1905. My father was a butcher and when they had anything special on, any big function, he was always there to help the butler. He did all the cutting of course. He always needed a messenger, so I was the messenger, and if he wanted anything I would go to fetch it for him. Elizabeth was just a little girl then. She was very nice – very playful. Her brother David was much the same. They were great pals, always playing together. She was a very pretty little girl. Her father, the Earl, was a homely person, and so was her mother. They mixed with all the people, and were very popular with them. It didn't matter where they were, at any function, they were always very courteous. One day I was at the Castle on business and I was speaking to the factor, Mr Lawson, and Elizabeth came up and asked me if I had ever been to the top of the Castle. I said yes, I had been, but I said it was a very wet, dull day and visibility was nil. So she said to Mr Lawson: 'Take Miss Bruce up to the castle roof and when you are bringing her down show her into all the rooms.' So I was escorted nearly all afternoon, going through all the rooms. My sister was the captain of the Girl Guides here in Kirriemuir. We got Elizabeth to start a company at Glamis, so we were often down there during that time. She has always been very popular in the neighbourhood.

Mrs Lilian Thrussell

Daughter of an estate worker at St Paul's Walden Bury in Hertfordshire, when the Queen Mother was growing up there.

I was the youngest in the family and the first story I remember hearing about Lady Elizabeth was when she held my sister. My mother had taken my sister out in the pram, and the nanny had got Lady Elizabeth in her pram, or walking, I don't know which. And Lady Elizabeth wanted to lift my sister and hold her. She called her 'the big dolly', the 'china dolly', and so mother obediently stayed and let her hold her. I also remember her well when she was courting and the Duke of York used to come to St Paul's Walden Bury. He came down for the shooting with Lord Strathmore, and we used to see him, almost always in a grey suit. He was a very nice gentleman; young and debonair. We were all excited, the people on the estate, because we used to wonder whether she would marry a royal prince. We were very fond of her, and of course it was romantic for her to marry a prince. She was so lovely and natural and people did like her.

There was a lot of excitement when they got engaged. We knew before it was announced. When they had a house party they always came to church, and that particular Sunday Lady Elizabeth was absent, and so was the Duke. I think they went for a walk instead. You read in these books that they got engaged in the garden, but I always think myself that he asked her on what is called 'The Walks'. It's an avenue of trees that goes on for miles, and you can see the house from the top. I think that's where he proposed to her, on that Sunday morning. Then the news came out that they were engaged to be married. There was great excitement. Everybody said, 'At last.' We were all very pleased that they seemed so happy together. It seemed as if they were made for each other.

In later years we used to see her too, because my husband was one of the church wardens at the little church at St Paul's Walden. The telephone used to go in our house and David, who was co-warden, used to say to my husband: 'Alfred, get the umbrella, Her Majesty's coming.' And he used to be in charge of a special cushion that she used to have on her seat for when she knelt down. It was always kept locked away. And when it was time, eleven o'clock, he used to go to the gate of the church and meet her, with the vicar, and escort her to her seat, bow, and that was that. Then go down when she signed the register after the service. She used to bring her detective with her, and he used to come in the evening and go up into the belfry and do bell ringing with my husband. He used to sing in the choir with my husband as well. It was a grand occasion. Everybody was happy together, which was the sort of atmosphere that this great lady always brings. She's got a most marvellous calming atmosphere about her. I think it's her depth of feeling for human nature to start with. And she has always got this ready smile for people and such a wonderful memory. She remembers everything, people's faces and so on, and she won't pass them. If they're there in the crowd she will pause, sometimes to have her picture taken. It's very sad to think that one day she won't be with us. I can't visualise St Paul's Walden without that feeling that she's going to come twice a year. She always comes to all the fêtes that we've had at the Bury. I just don't want to think of when that sad day will come. I will have to, but a great sadness will come over all of us.

Sir Fitzroy Maclean

At various times diplomat, soldier, Conservative MP, traveller and writer, Sir Fitzroy shared an ancient Scottish lineage with the Queen Mother, and was a regular weekend guest at Royal Lodge, Windsor.

I first met her when she was Duchess of York before the war. She came over, she and the Duke of York, for a St Andrew's Day ball in Paris. I was at the embassy in charge of the arrangements. She struck me then, and ever since, as enormously friendly, radiant, kind, outgoing and enjoying life.

I mean she is wonderful with people, always has been. I think that's something that comes from her Highland upbringing, which makes people naturally good with other people. The life of a child, at somewhere like Glamis, is really the perfect upbringing for anybody. I think in the Highlands there aren't the same barriers as there are in England and other parts of the country, and it meant that she had a wide circle of little friends from all walks of life early on. She was brought up to be nice to everybody, and that is something that has stayed with her. Certainly she is still deeply attached to Scotland; she's happiest of all in Scotland, and feels herself profoundly Scottish and a Highlander.

I think that the King depended on her in all kinds of ways. She was an enormous support to him. She also helped, as it were, bring him out and strengthen him in his convictions. She is a very strong character and one notices that all the time. However much fun she is, and however much she seems to be enjoying herself, you know that there is always this solid foundation and great natural goodness. That, I'm sure, was an enormous help to the King, who himself was a very good man, but inclined to be shy and withdrawn. And at the end of his life he relaxed more and more. She was also immensely important at the time of the

Abdication. She provided great steadiness, and after the trouble over Mrs Simpson and so on, that was what was needed. I was at the embassy in Paris at the time and therefore saw it in a slightly more detached way. But seeing it from that angle one realised exactly what was happening and was aware – by then having met her myself – how vitally important she was.

She was the perfect consort, although she would have been wonderful in whatever role that she had played in life. But at that particular moment she and the King together saved what could have been a dangerous situation. She has helped make the British monarchy one of the strongest there's ever been in history and the most popular.

Since then I have been fortunate enough to have been regularly invited to spend weekends at Royal Lodge where the atmosphere is always enormously jolly. She gets together once a year the same group of old friends and we have a wonderful time. Royal Lodge is a lovely place to stay and the food and drink is extremely good – she enjoys that, as we all do. Her Household are extremely well geared to this; indeed they join in. Then quite often the Queen comes over from Windsor Castle, and we have the happiest weekend you can imagine. There are a terrific lot of jokes and jolly stories, and not only is she great fun herself, but it's unbelievable what we talk about. She was born with the century, so she's quite an old lady, but it doesn't occur to you for a moment to think that. She's the youngest of the party. She likes every kind of joke and none of it is silly or stupid. Some of the people who are there have held great offices of State and so on, but they all relax and the conversation is very good indeed. She has this sort of inner vitality, this drive, and also a sweet nature, but not sugary sweet. She can be quite acerbic.

Queen Elizabeth has strong feelings on a number of subjects and makes it quite clear what they are, but I draw a definite veil over those. She has an enormous sense of humour, but again, far from sugary. In fact, very much to the point. She doesn't miss a trick. It's kindly meant when kindliness is deserved; not quite so kindly when it isn't. But basically she is very kind and understanding.

There's always lots of good English, or should we say, good

Sir Fitzroy Maclean, himself a traveller
on a grand scale, met the then Duchess of York
in Paris before the war.

British food, and always plenty to drink. There's even a certain amount of singing and story-telling. Everyone gathers round the piano, and some of the former Ministers of the Crown, ambassadors and all kinds of people sing – mostly old comic songs. Winston Churchill used to do the same; he used to love old music hall songs from the 1890s.

I remember one of her luncheon parties for a particular reason. I was going to appear on the television programme *This Is Your Life* and, as you know, the victim – if that's the word for it – doesn't know that anything is happening. I was told I was going to be on some chat programme about books. It didn't sound very interesting or very important. In the meantime all this research was going on round me which I was quite unaware of. I was at home in Scotland when the weather suddenly turned very fine, which it doesn't always do, and I rang up my wife, Veronica, who was in London, and said: 'I've decided not to come down after all for the week of the programme.' So she was thunderstruck and didn't know what to do. She knows when I make my mind up it stays made. So she rang up Martin Gilliat [the Queen Mother's then Private Secretary] and explained the problem, and he immediately said: 'We'll tell him Queen Elizabeth has got a jolly lunch party and see if that doesn't bring him down.' So he rang me up and I said of course I'd love to come down. I then rang up Veronica and said, 'Aren't we lucky, we've been asked to lunch with Queen Elizabeth. I'm coming down on the sleeper tonight.' Well, her luncheon parties are always great fun, and again there's plenty to eat and drink. I arrived at Clarence House and I thought perhaps the party was even more hilarious than usual. Of course, what I didn't realise was that everybody there knew what had happened, and why I'd been brought down, including, of course, my hostess. Then I went off to the programme which turned out to be *This Is Your Life.* There was a lot of teasing afterwards.

Canon John Treadgold

Became Chaplain at the Royal Chapel, Windsor Great Park, in 1981, and knew the Queen Mother well from her attendances at the Chapel whenever she was staying at Royal Lodge.

Queen Elizabeth is here at Royal Lodge nearly every weekend for certain times of the year, except when she is on holiday in Scotland. Coming to Royal Lodge is like coming home to her. She has been staying here ever since 1931, when she and the Duke of York, as he was then, came as reasonably young marrieds and made this their country home. The Princesses were brought up here, and spent most of their war years here and in the castle, which is about four miles away in the centre of Windsor. When she is here at weekends she comes to the Chapel; I see her there, and also a little bit after the service as well, informally, in Royal Lodge.

The Queen Mother takes a great deal of interest in the forms of the service, though the chapel in Windsor Great Park is the private chapel of the Queen. Even so, the Queen does defer a little bit to her mother. Obviously she is a relatively elderly lady and she is somewhat traditional, certainly where church services are concerned. So we use the Prayer Book, the 1928 version, which is the first amended version of the 1662 book. I think the idea of the alternative services book is a little anathema to her. About two years ago I did take a Lent course with a group of people here, and we looked at the liturgy of the church. We ended up by using the alternative services book for two celebrations, but then we reverted to the Prayer Book.

Queen Elizabeth hinted before we actually started that it was just an experiment, so there was no going back to her and saying: 'May we continue?' It was taken for granted, I think, that we would go on using the Prayer Book. She prefers to stick to the good old traditional service, which she has known and loved for many years. It's the same with the Bible. I was very rash when I first came here in 1981. I had used the Revised Standard Version Bible for many years and did so for my first service. I read that wonderful description from the Old Testament of the visit of the Queen of Sheba to Solomon, and afterwards Queen Elizabeth said to me: 'What a lovely story that is, Chaplain,' and I said: 'Yes, ma'am.' She then looked at me with a lovely smile and said: 'Yes, in my version such lovely words.' We had a laugh together, but I took the point.

Again, a few years ago I asked if we might introduce *A Hundred Hymns for Today*. 'Yes, certainly,' came the reply. 'But not too many new tunes.' In many ways I think she is just echoing what a lot of people feel.

She has a very traditional, uncomplicated faith, which is supportive in her life. I don't think she is terribly interested in the subtleties of theology, especially those expounded in some quarters today. In the Royal Chapel we pray for her and for the Queen and other members of the Royal Family, and also for people who work here on the estate. I think this means something to her. She uses a super prayer book; an enormous one which she has open in front of her. She also uses a very small prayer book – there must be very few of them about – which has in it a prayer for Edward the King, referring to King Edward VIII. On one occasion when we were talking after the service, she asked me why we prayed for the Prince and Princess of Wales, and not Prince Charles by name. I looked at her and she smiled back very graciously, and I said: 'I am required to do so by lawful authority, ma'am.' And she said: 'Well, in my prayer book it is Albert, Duke of York, and the Duchess of York,' indicating that she thought I ought to pray for Charles, Prince of Wales, and the Princess of Wales. So now we are doing that; both here in the Great Park and in St George's Chapel we pray for Charles, Prince of Wales, and the Princess of Wales.

I think her faith must have sustained her greatly at the time of the King's death. I know how concerned she is with people who suffer bereavement. There was a man who had been chef to Queen

Elizabeth and King George VI, who now lives in retirement in Old Windsor here. He comes up to Royal Lodge occasionally to help out when they have large house parties. His wife died a few weeks ago and he had a most marvellous letter from Queen Elizabeth. Obviously she was very concerned for him, and I think appreciated very deeply what he was going through at that particular time. This letter, two pages in her own hand, helped him enormously.

She likes a little bit of gossip occasionally too, and is always interested if I am in a position to tell her about people on the estate, their families, what they are doing and even their animals. She smiles with her eyes and her mouth, and seems to listen with her eyes as well. You can see that she is deeply interested. She is very gracious, but terribly honest and straightforward, and also very determined. If she wants something, or she would like you to do something, it's always: 'Do you think you could possibly ...?' She is in no way a dictator. If she invites me into Royal Lodge she will never say: 'Would you come in.' It's: 'Have you got the time?' or 'Would you care to?' Her whole attitude endears her to so many people, but underneath it there is this strain of determination. She knows what she wants, she sees the goal posts and they're not moved to suit a situation. The goal posts are there and she helps people towards them in the nicest possible way.

The Marchioness of Salisbury

Noted gardener, whose skill in renovating the gardens at her husband's family home, Hatfield House, has been widely recognised. She is the author of a book on the Queen Mother's gardens at Clarence House, Birkhall, Royal Lodge and the Castle of Mey.

Her gardens are all very different, but they are united by the taste of Queen Elizabeth and the different flowers, trees and shrubs that she is particularly interested in. So there is a sort of consistent theme running through each of the gardens which is really her character. Above all, she loves the old-fashioned flowers, and traditional gardening. I think it stems from her childhood because both her mother and grandmother were great gardeners, and lovers of plants. She remembers fondly certain plants from her childhood and flowers that she had an affection for, and grows them in her own gardens. You find them in all four of the gardens, things like the old-fashioned roses, lilies, and pansies, which are a particular love of hers and also of the late King's. Between them they made a pansy garden at Sandringham. I think her interests were broadened considerably when the King and she went to Royal Lodge and developed the garden there. They worked very closely with Sir Eric Saville, the man who developed the gardens now known as the Saville Gardens at Windsor. He was a wonderfully knowledgeable plantsman and gardener, and they planted many of the things that were being planted by him in the Saville Gardens, in the Royal garden. They included rhododendrons and azaleas, which were of particular interest to the late King. Queen Elizabeth really loves anything scented.

The Queen Mother and the Marchioness of Salisbury in the garden at the Castle of Mey.

The Castle of Mey has a very special charm, and I think it is special in another way because it was the first house and garden that was really hers. It was found and chosen by her. The garden which was already there was tremendously neglected and needed a lot of resuscitation. It was within a great wall, and was an old-fashioned cottage garden, typical of the gardens attached to Scottish castles. She has done something very remarkable there, because the conditions are all against gardening – the wind blows pretty well the whole year round, and although the climate isn't very severe it seems to be, because of this great wind. It's quite difficult to find things that will flourish and stand upright against it. Yet she has succeeded in recreating a delightful old-fashioned cottage garden. Vegetables and fruit are grown with the flowers, mingled in a way that used to be done in the sixteenth and seventeenth centuries. It would be almost impossible without that great wall. It's difficult enough with it. The gardener there told me that he'd seen a mighty cabbage plucked off its stalk and carried over the fifteen-foot wall by the wind, so you can imagine what they have to battle against there.

At Birkhall, too, the vegetables are very prominent indeed, and very beautiful, like the curly kale, the blue and red cabbages, and the rows of blue-green leeks, all edged by borders of charming flowers, which is one of the things Queen Elizabeth is very fond of. Or perhaps a clipped white heather hedge, surrounding rows of peas and beans and her beloved sweet peas. I remember the gardener telling me that he grew what he called 'proper' sweet peas behind the potting shed, up bamboo canes, with nice long stalks for picking for the house. But what Queen Elizabeth loved was the medley of sweet peas just growing any-old-how on the pea sticks, again probably something she remembered from her childhood.

The garden of Clarence House is very much groomed and prepared for certain events, notably Trooping the Colour. The bedding-out and borders in the garden are prepared particularly for that moment when Queen Elizabeth has to entertain, but a gravel drive runs right through it. When the ambassadors or the visiting royalties come to call on Queen Elizabeth they have to use the gate which brings them up the drive and round to the portico. The drive rather circumscribes the development of the garden and Queen Elizabeth, who dislikes the gravel, has tried to narrow it down as much as possible, but enough has to be left for the carriage wheels. And so in a way it is not a garden you can develop to your own likes.

She is a creative force because she knews what she likes, and she talks to her gardeners and tells them what she would like to grow. She is also a worker in the garden, though obviously not so much in later years. She used to work in the rock garden at Birkhall, collecting plants from the wild and transplanting them into the rock garden. And she would do a bit of weeding. I have no doubt that if she'd had the time she would have been a real working gardener. She has a great love for actually doing things in the gardens.

As a person she is very warm and loving, she has got a great heart and perpetual interest in other people. You feel that she really is genuinely interested in you and anything that is affecting you. She has a most generous spirit, and, of course, this tremendously endearing thing of being able to make people laugh, an enjoyment of life and sparkling good humour. She's very entertaining and you feel the whole room livens up and a special sparkle comes when she arrives. She makes everybody feel on top form, which is a great and rare art. She also has this wonderful gift of putting people at their ease, making them feel that they can be themselves and be absolutely natural with her. But although she is an amusing and sparkling person, there is still enormous depth to her. To me she is completely unique. She has tremendous strength of character, but always a feeling that she is a very loving and understanding person.

Prince Jean-Louis de Faucigny-Lucingz

Member of an ancient French family, whose connections gave him access to most of the country's great houses. He arranged for the Queen Mother to stay privately in a succession of them, and was a member of the party on her foreign travels for many years.

I first met Queen Elizabeth many years ago, before the war when she was Duchess of York. My mother-in-law had a house in Piccadilly next door to her, and my two elder daughters were more or less the same age as the present Queen and Princess Margaret. So, in order that they should learn French, the four of them used to go in the little garden which was at the disposal of all the tenants. So of course there were some social contacts. Then during the war I was at our Mission in Britain so I had the pleasure of seeing the Queen Mother, as Queen at that time, together with King George VI. She was very kind to the French. Then later, in about 1970, I had the pleasure and honour of being in a country house with her, and she said she adored France and she'd like to go back. She had come several times with a very old mutual friend, but he was then tired and old and couldn't travel any more. So I said: 'Oh, but if Your Majesty will allow I will arrange a journey.' So that's how it started. Then I became a kind of travel agent for her stays in France and we visited a great number of houses. I always chose lovely houses to stay in. There was no difficulty finding them because she's so popular and loved in France that everybody was always delighted to open their house to her and have her as a guest.

We've always travelled in exactly the same little group for all those years; the Duke and Duchess of Grafton, Sir Ralph

Anstruther, Lady Fermoy and myself. Exactly the same, it doesn't change, so we know each other's habits. We've visited most parts of France now. She loves sightseeing and I always arrange that in advance with great care. She also likes seeing people in their houses, so I make sure there is always a village nearby. Everywhere we've been, we've always managed to organise going to lunch or dinner in some other nice place, and then we've gone on to visit some monument, church, or place of historical interest, which she enjoys a lot.

When we first arrive people are delighted, but probably sometimes a little nervous. Not for long though; she's such a charmer. It's that extraordinary natural niceness she has, and then that kindness. She takes an interest in everyone and everything and has a natural curiosity. She wants to know all about the history of the place and all about the family. When we are to meet people, she likes to know about them in advance. I think her love of France is in her Scots blood. There are great links between France and Scotland; there always have been for reasons I've never fathomed. I suppose it's on account of the Stuarts, ever since Mary Stuart, anyway. I have always been struck when I'm in Scotland that so many Scots speak perfect French. She often expresses her love for France. For instance this year we went to Sicily. We always plan in advance, so I said: 'What about next year, Your Majesty?' and she said: 'Oh, you know, I miss France a lot.' So that made me understand that she'd like to come back.

She is very popular with the French people – adored. When we're in France there's not a village we pass where people are not at their windows or in the street waving to her. I think she's about the most popular person I know, and in France certainly. In France our visits are really kept very private so there's a minimum of official demands. The Sicilian trip was different. The very fact that we were on a large yacht like the *Britannia* made it so. Her Majesty doesn't mind that because I think it also has a very good propaganda value. It was good for Britain when we arrived in the ports. There were official visits, but she's got such a way with her on these occasions that I don't think she's unhappy. It's part of what she considers her job, and she does it beautifully. The people who go to things with her are more tired than she is.

Prince Jean-Louis de Faucigny-Lucingz with the Queen Mother during one of her private visits to France.

Two things give her her vitality; her curiosity, and then her natural good health. She's extraordinary. I've never heard her say: 'I'm going to have a rest,' or something like that. She also has a great sense of fun and she doesn't miss a trick. She sees through people very well indeed. She's got a strong character and a great idea of her mission and role, which is quite right. On our journeys I've never seen anyone become familiar with her; they wouldn't do it because she inspires natural respect in people.

She was on *Britannia* when she went to Venice three years ago and I went to join her there. *Britannia* was going back to England because it had been, if I remember, to Trieste with the Prince of Wales on an official visit, and it stopped for three days so that she could stay aboard. She had come for the Save Venice Fund, to see the work that had been done. She told me that the only other time she'd been to Venice was when she and the Duke of York went to the wedding of Prince Paul of Yugoslavia and Princess Olga. They were on the Orient Express, which at that time stopped for half an hour in the station in Venice. So they got out of the train, but all they saw of Venice was the platform in front of the station, and at the top of the step they saw the canal, very dirty at that point and very messy. That's all she'd seen of Venice till happily she saw it in better conditions from *Britannia*. Unfortunately the weather wasn't very good. But she loved it.

I have a great respect for Queen Elizabeth; great admiration for her and for her qualities and, if I dare use the word, great affection. I have come to appreciate more and more over the years her increasing kindness and friendship. That friendship, which honours and flatters me, is an element of my life which I appreciate immensely.

Comte et Comtesse de Nicolay

Owners of the spectacular chateau, Le Lude, between Tours and Le Mans in the Loire Valley, where the Queen Mother stayed.

COMTE DE NICOLAY:

It's a very big souvenir for us that the Queen Mother came to our home. It was a glorious day which the local population and my family will never forget. The sun arrived just the day before she came, and the rain came the day after she left. So we spent four marvellous days with her. She was absolutely charming with the population, speaking French to everybody, and asking news of everyone she met. She was a marvellous guest, walking with us, speaking with my children, and my brother and my sister-in-law, and living with us without any difficulties. I must confess I was not very relaxed before I received the Queen Mother, but after one day speaking with her it was absolutely relaxed.

When she was here, first of all she wanted to see the *son et lumière*, which is very famous in France. It is performed by the people of the village. We see the house in the background and the actors play the history of the house and the gardens. She enjoyed it very much. After it had finished at midnight, we invited quite a lot of friends of ours to the house, and the Queen Mother stayed up till two o'clock in the morning, speaking and chatting with them and there was a very nice ambiance. She particularly likes young people, and she was speaking a great deal with them after the *son et lumière*.

Comtesse de Nicolay:

My memories are two days of big feasting and big organisation. We had a lot of friends who came to see the Queen Mother, and we took her to a lot of other villages near here. For us it was like a fairy story; like in a film or something very special. She is very *bon vivant*, as we say in French. We gave her products of the country, special fish from our river and wine from our land, and I think she liked them. I think the family was nervous at the beginning, though I was not there. I arrived when everything had already started and the atmosphere was relaxed and very happy, so I didn't really live the moments before her arrival.

Sir Hugh Casson

Architect, artist and former President of the Royal Academy. He became a friend of the Queen Mother's through her interest in paintings.

I first got to know Queen Elizabeth when I became President of the Royal Academy and we used regularly to ask her, as a great lover of pictures, to come to see whatever was on. We would give small lunches and dinners for her. Gradually this grew into closer contacts, like going to stay at Royal Lodge, Windsor, where she used to have weekends for poets and writers and musicians, to which my wife and I were lucky enough to be asked. Then we all started going each year to the King's Lynn Festival as her guests, followed by brief holidays in Italy, Sicily and France, and that's how it gradually warmed up into friendship.

Queen Elizabeth has always been interested in paintings. If you go into her house the pictures are leaning against sofas and propped up against walls and sitting on chairs, which means that the owner of them is really looking at them, wondering perhaps where to hang them: 'Shall we change it?' or 'Where shall we put this one?', and isn't just worried about getting them on a nail. I think this is always a sign of a genuine interest in and love of pictures. And again what I like is the breadth of her choice; Lely or Sickert, Sisley, Monet or Wilson, Steer, Sargent or Sidney Nolan. There's a difference between 'collecting' things and 'liking' things. If you are a collector I think you tend to fit them into little gaps in your collection, and what I like about her collection is that it is so tremendously varied. In her rooms there isn't a feeling that you are going into the eighteenth-century room of a gallery. It is a lovely mixture of stuff. And the whole room is covered with dog-leads and china and newspapers and magazines

Sir Hugh Casson and the Queen Mother out for a Sunday afternoon walk in Windsor Great Park.

and flowers and diaries and waste-paper baskets, and dogs themselves, too. So it's a good country-house background – an affectionate muddle she seems to enjoy and create round her.

I don't think we have ever discussed it, but I would guess that she would find it difficult to accept and enjoy abstract painting. I have never seen any in her house. Now everybody knows it's not easy to love abstract art and you've got to work at it, but if you're working as hard as Queen Elizabeth at other things, you haven't got much time to work at getting to know about abstract paintings.

She has a lot of connections with music. She was President of the Royal College of Music, of which I'm a Member of Council, and was always a serious and responsible attender. At Windsor weekends she nearly always has a recently qualified student to play for the guests, and she goes to all their degree days and concerts. She has a genuine interest in music. I suppose like all girls of her class and upbringing of that period, she learned to play the piano. I don't think she herself ever paints, though several members of the family do with considerable skill.

Being royal is a terrible handicap in so many ways. I remember Queen Elizabeth saying when we were in Sicily that you can't go into any gallery anywhere and look at a picture without somebody with the best of intentions explaining it to you. You can't go in and say to your companion: 'That's rather nice,' or 'Isn't that dreadful?' because you've always got the director of the gallery or the chief art historian for Italy standing by you rolling out facts, which are not always interesting and are often distracting. All you really want to do is just look at it yourself in quiet and silence, and that, I think, is very difficult for them. Of course, she never shows it for a second, but I sense that it is a trial. You don't want everything explained to you all the time, even by the top people. But this hazard has never diminished her appetite for sightseeing. It is impossible to diminish her appetite for anything. She's so extraordinary in the width and the variety of her interests, and her physical endurance in pursuing them. Whether it's going to the stud farm or to an art gallery, going to the opera or for a walk with the dogs early in the morning before breakfast, it is all absolutely non-stop.

Take our Sicilian trip, for instance, on *Britannia*. It was a private not a State visit, lasting five days. We left the ship at about ten in the morning and got back about five, having either driven or walked all day, except for lunch, looking at palaces and churches and temples and Greek theatres. And Queen Elizabeth, as you know, wears fairly high heels and the pavements of archaeological sites are not smooth, so it must have been very exhausting. But never a sign of this, and at six-thirty every evening she'd give a party on the ship for all the local dignitaries, and at eight-thirty it would be a dinner party, and at midnight she'd have the officers in from the wardroom for a last drink before going to bed. She couldn't even nod off in the car, because you're driving through cheering villages most of the time and if you're all sitting dozing in the back of the cars, it doesn't look too good. It is typical of her consideration for others that the driver is always instructed to reduce the speed when crowds are there to greet her.

She went down fantastically well with the Italian people. Sicily's a very uneasy place in some people's view, and we obviously had a lot of police presence. But Queen Elizabeth said that she never worried in Italy because they always love grannies: 'They'd never touch the hair of a granny's head.' So she always felt perfectly safe.

Another nice thing about Italians is they always give great pride of place to the children. If you go to a very posh dinner or lunch, in a huge palace, with princes and dukes and footmen and all the rest of it, there'll always be the family children in party-frocks scudding around your ankles and screeching. Italians always take the children as part of life, as they take art as part of life, which is one of the pleasures of going to Italy.

When we go to the King's Lynn Festival we stay at Sandringham. It is always very relaxed when Queen Elizabeth is there, though I think she likes formality and enjoys the sort of rhythm and system of it. She has very efficient courtiers and people who shepherd you round so that you don't make ludicrous mistakes and sit in her favourite chair. But it is relaxed because she is a wonderfully relaxed person, and always so happy-looking. It's a commonplace thing to say, but happy faces are not all that usual in fact. If you walk down the street, have people got happy faces?

They're thoughtful sometimes, but so often they're just unlively. Queen Elizabeth's face is always very lively and mobile. Mind you, I don't think she has ever seen an unhappy face herself. I would guess that all her life she has been loved, and wherever she goes people love to see her, so she has always seen people smiling. This, I think, is a terrific injection. I mean, if you're tired and you come into a room and everybody's noticeably glad to see you (which is an experience not all of us have very often) it must give you a welcome lift.

I think she is devoted to human relationships, and she is wonderful at them. She is also good at disengaging too, which is difficult for a very friendly person. I remember introducing her to an American lady at St James's Palace, and before you knew where you were, the American lady was pulling out photographs of her children, pressing them on her and saying: 'Do please keep them.' Of course, she wouldn't say: 'Well it's been terribly sweet of you but ...' so instead she took them and stuffed them in her bag. She has to circulate and that's where the problem of disengagement comes in. We all know what it's like, because we all get stuck with somebody at a party, and you think up all the excuses, like saying: 'I must go and rescue my wife,' and then you find that your wife's talking to her husband. With the Royal Family, where everybody wants to meet you, you mustn't get too interested, however interested you are. You've got to move on. And doing that politely and easily in a way which people respond to is very difficult. Particularly because she has that extraordinary quality of making you feel you're the only person in the room she wants to talk to. You really feel that she is genuinely pleased to see you, and genuinely sad to lose you. To help ease the moment of separation she has a little sort of raising of one hand that says: 'Ah well, that's the way it goes.' It's not quite a good-bye but a statement of regret in which both sides share.

At Sandringham dinner is usually about half past eight, and goes on till about ten. And then quite often, nearly always in fact, there is a bit of music afterwards, because one of the ladies-in-waiting, Lady Fermoy, is the President of the King's Lynn Festival and virtually a professional pianist. We also sometimes have a bit of singing, anything from old Noël Coward to whatever has been stored since Queen Alexandra's time in the music stool. It might be 'Come into the garden, Maud' or Cole Porter, or if there are professional musicians there, which quite often happens, then they play seriously late into the night.

It's always interesting to remember that she was born when Queen Victoria was still alive. I heard a terribly sad remark the other day. Somebody said: 'Now that Mrs Thompson's gone there's nobody left to call me Nellie.' It's a familiar experience to all of us when we get into old age. More and more people who called her 'Nellie', so to speak, are no longer alive. But luckily all Queen Elizabeth's old friends seem, despite their age, to be almost as active as she is, and so indeed is her Household. In the normal royal service you retire at between sixty and sixty-five, but Queen Elizabeth doesn't obey this rule. Being independent, she keeps her staff on as long as they want to be there.

The two things that seem to stick in the mind about her are her slight sense of mischief and her instant friendliness to people. She'd be walking, for instance, through a field and meet a hiker or farmhand, and whereas most of us would just say 'Hello,' or 'Good afternoon,' she would nearly always stop and engage them in a bit of conversation: 'Do you come from around these parts?' – totally unnecessary friendliness, but so deeply part of her that it shines in her face. It is a very elusive face, and although she's beautiful, she's apparently very difficult to paint. I know of no successful portrait, except a very early one when she was about fifteen or sixteen, done I suppose when she was more quiet and restrained and shy. The Augustus John one is a disaster. Of course, all painters get self-conscious when painting royalty. The stakes are so high. Portrait painting is very difficult, particularly with people like Queen Elizabeth whose expressions flit like cloud shadows across a pond, like ripples that cross and come back again. You try to catch it, but it's gone. Its charm lies in its mobility. It's a nightmare. Photographers can catch it sometimes, and I think quite a lot of the photographers have managed to do this, but I don't think I've ever yet seen a really successful portrait of her – I know one painter who destroyed two attempts. I am told Augustus John wanted to destroy his too. Perhaps he was frightened, although she couldn't have been a less frightening person. She confessed to having talked all the time she was being painted, to make him feel at ease.

If I were to choose an image for Queen Elizabeth, I would choose a wave breaking on a rock, because though she is sweet and pretty and charming, she also has a basic streak of toughness and tenacity. You know when a wave breaks on a rock, it showers and sparkles with a brilliant play of foam and droplets in the sun, yet beneath is really hard, tough rock, fused, in her case, from strong principles, physical courage and a sense of duty. And I think it's this balance between the tenacity and shrewdness, plus the sparkle which is always present, which makes the attraction of Queen Elizabeth so absolutely unique.

The Earl of Lichfield

Professional photographer and great-nephew of the Queen Mother. Her brother was his grandfather on his mother's side.

We were brought up to a large extent during the war in a house in Windsor, and as we grew up we were asked to the Castle. I remember going to pantomimes that took place there, but more particularly I recall the dancing classes, which were run by a wonderful old lady who used to make us go through all those perfectly useless dances, which one never uses again, like the polka. Queen Elizabeth was always there, and she was extremely caring and kind. I remember being rather awed by this enormous room in which we were all doing these little steps. She was always the person who came to pick one up if one fell

The Earl of Lichfield.

over. I never dreamt that I might go back as a tradesman later on – to take pictures of the family. I remember one occasion when I had to be dragged screaming out of her car, because I'd got into it after being a page at a wedding. I'd come out with the bride, and then leapt into the nearest car, which was not mine but hers!

When it comes to photographing her it's rather easy. One can see she has this expression, a sort of wonderful smile she produces, but also she is the only person in a group you never have to look at to see if she's looking right, because she always is. I suppose it's years of practice and great confidence. Something seems to come from within her, which is very helpful for us photographers, whereas it's probably more difficult for painters. The true test of whether you can catch an expression is not so much when you are photographing someone who is posing, but when one is a press photographer working in the street. If you look at the press photographs of her they're nearly always wonderful. When I first started in Fleet Street a press photographer told me that she was easily the most reliable person to photograph. If she was reviewing or inspecting a line of troops, she was so good at it that we figured she used to actually stop about six men from the end so that you got a full length, and then she'd stop two from the end so we got a close-up.

She is quite at ease being photographed, especially if you're quick. That's probably the case with all the Royal Family, so long as you're quick and you go for it. She also puts one very much at one's ease, as indeed she does with everyone. I think the interesting thing is the informality that she manages to exude. Sometimes after dinner when I've been with her she will start a sing-song, which is marvellously cosy. It tends to be the songs that I learnt at my mother's knee, which she learnt from her father, who was Queen Elizabeth's brother. So the songs stem from Glamis and all the Bowes Lyon background. She still remembers all the words, although I forget them.

Lord Annan

Former Vice-Chancellor of London University, he came to know the Queen Mother well when she was Chancellor of the university.

My earliest memories of Queen Elizabeth are when I was a child. I was taken to a stand in Whitehall and I heard the clip-clop of the horses as the carriages bowled down Whitehall taking Elizabeth Bowes Lyon to her wedding. But of course, it was when she was Chancellor of the University of London and I was Vice-Chancellor that I really got to known her. In her role as Chancellor she was serene and wonderfully approachable, putting everybody at their ease. But more than that, whenever she visited a place, a college, or a medical school, the whole morale of the place shot up. She had that gift of encouraging people simply by being there and taking an interest in what they did. She was not at all shy, she genuinely opened out to people and produced an atmosphere of calm. Everybody is nervous when a royal visit takes place, because they always think that something terrible is going to happen. I remember she got stuck in a lift in the Senate House, and it took some time to release her, but she took it entirely in her stride, and made a joke about it. Indeed, sometimes I feel that because things go so smoothly with royal visits there is nothing royalty likes more than a good bust-up, where things go hopelessly wrong and they can have a good giggle about it. She was very much like that. She was enchanting in her conversation because you didn't have to try and find some subject, like racing, for example, to interest her. She was interested in what you were doing, I don't mean personally, but I mean the university as a whole. Her role wasn't very formal, in the sense of governing anything. I think she did once accept an invitation to preside at a meeting of the Senate, but directly she sat down in her chair, she turned to the Vice-Chancellor and asked him to conduct the business. That wasn't her role; her role in the university was visiting every institution in the place, and there are a lot of institutions in the University of London. She knew everything, she knew the people who ran them – she has, of course, a remarkable memory.

The other thing that made the University of London sympathetic to her is its association with the Commonwealth. Half the universities in the Commonwealth owe something to the University of London. The Commonwealth is very dear to Queen Elizabeth's heart; she belongs to the age of the British Empire and you felt this.

She would never interfere on a matter of policy, but sometimes she did express her slight sadness that some change had to be made. One must be quite honest about this – Queen Elizabeth is not one who delights in change for its own sake. She is very conservative in her views and she likes things to be as she has always known them. So, when the time came when we had to amalgamate colleges and make economies of all kinds, she was not very happy.

I remember when I took the decision to sell the university press. It used to be called the Athlone Press after the Earl of Athlone who had been the Chancellor before Queen Elizabeth and indeed was a member of the Royal Family. The Queen Mother was very alarmed that the press would lose its identity, but I was able to reassure her on that, and say: 'No, it has been bought by another firm and they are going to maintain the imprint.' That set her mind at rest, but of course she didn't like it.

You did get the message if she wanted something done. In my experience such messages didn't arise very often – the only message one got was 'Please have the gin-and-tonic waiting at a particular moment, and try not to serve her wine before dinner.' When she did want something she would just lift her eyebrows slightly and give you a quizzical look as if to say: 'I wonder if you could do that.' And you knew you ought to do it! She had a way with her that was part of her great magic.

She is also a woman of some determination. You knew perfectly

Lord Annan with the Queen Mother
at London University in 1977.

well if the Queen Mother didn't like something. There was no doubt about it. But it wasn't done in terms of being sniffy or sulky or anything like that, far from it. She simply had a way of slightly indicating if things could be done this way rather than that way. Of course, she has been in many a difficult position. I can well remember – nothing to do with the University of London – that some dignitary in the House of Commons got rather, shall we say, tired and over-emotional, and to see the Queen Mother disentangle herself from his advances was really a lesson in courtly and firm behaviour.

I'm sure she enjoyed her time at the university. She felt that she was, after all, head of a very great institution. She loves people, especially young people, and was frightfully good with them. She also liked meeting people from a very different walk of life. And she was so enchanting in the way she would greet any expression of enthusiasm with equanimity. I remember the head of the college suddenly marching up, seizing her by the hand and kissing it in, shall we say, a somewhat over-enthusiastic demonstration of loyalty. But to the Queen Mother that was a case of what she sometimes called 'charming enthusiasm'. She also rather enjoyed the processions of academics. They do look very curious – like a lot of crabs moving sideways.

I shall always remember her laughter, and when one went to Clarence House being astonished at how hearty her appetite was. The lunches at Clarence House were both extremely good and extremely formidable, course after course of good, sound, hearty English fare, and most enjoyable it was.

(*Above*) A portrait by the photographer Cecil Beaton taken in 1956, four years after the King's death.

(*Previous page*) One of a series of dramatic backdrops devised for the Queen by Cecil Beaton in 1948.

(*Above*) Derby Day, Epsom Racecourse 1962.

(*Left*) The Queen Mother leaves St George's Chapel with Prince Charles after the Garter Ceremony in 1968.

(*Opposite*) Photographed with a sumptuous background by Cecil Beaton in 1970.

(*Previous page*) By the late 1950s Elizabeth had settled into the role of Queen Mother, which she was to occupy for decades to come.

(*Left and below*) More from Cecil Beaton's portfolio of the Queen Mother at 70.

At the Ideal Home Exhibition in 1978.

(*Overleaf*) The Queen joins in the public celebrations of her mother's 80th birthday outside Clarence House.

Mrs Peter Cazalet

Her late husband was the first trainer of the Queen Mother's horses, at Fairlawne, in Kent. After his death the Queen Mother regularly invited Mrs Cazalet to stay at Birkhall.

I first got to know Queen Elizabeth in any sort of friendship when she trained with my husband at Fairlawne. She was a wonderful owner, as you can imagine, and it lifted up the whole stable, everyone adored her so much.

Her very first horse was called Monaveen. It was shared by the Queen and the then Princess Elizabeth. That got her really interested and from then onwards she never looked back. There's quite an amusing little story – I can't remember if the present Queen was Queen then – but anyway, my husband asked Princess Margaret once if she thought that the next horse was going to be shared. And Princess Margaret said: 'Oh, no, Mummy wouldn't share with anybody now.' By that time she wanted to have the full glory.

The relationship between my husband and her was very close. He would have done a Sir Walter Raleigh for her and enjoyed it much more than Sir Walter Raleigh did, I'm sure. She used to come and stay with us at Fairlawne and would race on Friday and Saturday. I think her first visit for a weekend was in 1956. She came every year for about sixteen years, to stay for the Lingfield Park meeting. We invited different people for her, but hardly ever horsey people because she saw enough of those racing each day. For instance, we had Noël Coward and it was such a success that we had him, if not twice running, then with just a year in between. She was wonderful with him, encouraging him to play and sing, and knowing all his tunes. It was: 'Do play this, oh, do play that, oh, how wonderful.'

She's got a terrific sense of humour. I remember we had some people we'd met in Tahiti. One of them was the daughter of James Hall who wrote *Mutiny on the Bounty*. And he, the chap, brought a nail from the *Bounty* and gave it to Queen Elizabeth. Noël Coward was there at the time and he said afterwards: 'Ma'am, if you'd seen your face when he presented you with that nail that he'd had put in a Cartier box, and you said: "Oh, a nail."' And of course she roared with laughter, just as much as all of us.

I remember one occasion when she came down just for the day. She always used to come alone; no lady-in-waiting or anything like that. We were down at the stables, and totally unprompted my youngest son, who was then thirteen, came in. He has always been car-mad, and I think a car had been abandoned in a drive and he'd said: 'Papa can I have that car, can I put it together, can I buy this, can I buy that?' It was an awful, dirty thing but he adored it. He used to drive me around all the time in the park, and in the home woods. Anyway, he arrived at the stables, and I said: 'Oh. Ma'am, here's Anthony with his car that he worships.' So of course, she said: 'Oh, how lovely that car is.' And he said: 'Would you like me to drive you in it?' Before I could say: 'Please Ma'am don't,' she had said: 'Of course I'd like it.' So she got in. I don't think it had any springs – you were literally sitting on the floor. We had lovely mown drives in the home woods at Fairlawne, and he drove her all round there. We kept saying: 'Where are they? Where are they?' But at last they came back, both smiling radiantly.

She has a quality which people respond to. When you're talking to her, you think that you're the only person that she wants to talk to. There's a sort of communication between her eyes and your eyes that gives you that impression. You're not only flattered, but very honoured. It's a unique quality – I don't know anybody else who has it, royal or not. It's not just because she's royal that I'm saying this, it's herself, her magic, an inward sort of sunshine.

As I said, she always used to come on her own to Fairlawne; no lady-in-waiting, though she would bring her dresser. She also brought a page, who is really a footman. People might think this would be difficult, but it's very convenient because he would tell the butler or the chef what time and what she wanted for breakfast, and he would carry it up and give it to her dresser. Then he would wait in the hall when one came in, and he would take her gloves and her scarf so none of it would be muddled up with anybody else's.

She knew everyone in the stables by name. When my husband died she came down to Fairlawne, and she saw all the stable lads who'd looked after any of her horses and had a little chat and gave them something, an ashtray with the royal crest or something. It's

Mrs Peter Cazalet (centre) with the Queen Mother and Princess Margaret at Hurst Park Races in 1959.

something they'll never forget, and that is so typical of Queen Elizabeth, because she thinks of everything.

She was wonderful after my husband died, because she understood. It's only if you've been through a thing like that that you can really understand the nightmare and the misery, and she went through it to the full because she worshipped the King. She wrote me many letters and sent flowers. Her heart is a very big heart.

When she comes to this little house in London it is sheer delight. She's got a remarkable memory. She sees things here that she used to see at Fairlawne, and says: 'Oh, I do remember that,' and she remembers where they were at Fairlawne. Very few people, in fact I don't think any of my other friends, would actually remember where things were, but Queen Elizabeth remembers.

She's very Scottish. I mean deep down she adores Scotland, and I am lucky enough to go and stay with her every year at Birkhall, on the Balmoral estate. She's really at home there. One of her favourite places is the lovely hut by the river that a lot of her family and friends gave her. I was privileged to be asked to contribute to it. We go there and have huge picnics, and if it's cold we make a fire. Queen Elizabeth contributes to all that and helps unpack. Then we carry chairs and tables and things out of doors.

We also often go out to tea. I remember once four of us went – Queen Elizabeth, a lady-in-waiting who drove the Land Rover, one other person and myself. We were driving along on a rough track when we suddenly came upon a huge piece of wire rolled up. The lady-in-waiting drove straight for it, and it got entangled in the wheels, and was impossible to disentangle. In pelting rain we all got out to push – Queen Elizabeth too – but finally we had to abandon it. We eventually had to go to a nearby cottage where one of the estate workers lived. So we ate our picnic there and eventually someone came and fetched us.

Staying at Birkhall is very relaxed; you could be staying with anybody. Obviously your manners are slightly better, and you curtsey in the morning and when you come down to dinner and when you go to bed.

After dinner Queen Elizabeth puts on the gramophone, and

gramophone it jolly well is, nothing modern, and we dance reels. I remember the last time, it was an eightsome – you have eight people round and you all dance with each other and it seems to take an eternity, particularly if you don't know how to do it, which I didn't. I was absolutely exhausted after it, but Queen Elizabeth was still full of energy, and when you dance with her she's like a feather. She has the most amazing stamina.

We once were lucky enough to go with her for a little trip on *Britannia*. She was going down to the Scilly Isles on a semi-official visit and we got on board somewhere down near Cornwall. We only went to half the places she did, but she would helicopter from one island to the other, and then when we got back on board we would be told to be ready in ten minutes, because there were people coming for drinks. Then we had to be ready in a quarter of an hour for twenty people for dinner. After four or five days we were exhausted, but when we sailed into Portsmouth she was still as fresh as a daisy. When we got on the train to come to London with her, she asked if we'd like lunch at Clarence House. We said no, we couldn't because we had to go to bed. We were so exhausted, and we'd only done half what she did.

She is a very strong character and a very disciplined person; she's got this wonderful light and heavenly smile, but my word, I'm sure she can be very determined. Her principles are rigid and, I'm convinced, always right, because she's that sort of person. She's a profoundly good person, which shows in her face.

She writes the most beautiful letters; they're masterpieces. The most wonderful letters I've ever had in my life are from Queen Elizabeth – be it thanking me for a dinner, or when my husband died. They are of deep feeling and beautifully phrased. Knowing her has been a great honour and a great privilege. A lot of people obviously know her very much better than I do, but I do consider I know her well, and I really do adore her. Certainly it made the whole difference to my husband, and it has to me; it's uplifted my life.

The Black Watch

The Queen Mother had connections with many units of the armed services, but the Black Watch, the regiment of her father, her uncles and her brothers, was always considered her favourite.

The Queen Mother's first public engagement after the death of King George VI in 1952 was to visit the Black Watch in Fife. She inspected soldiers from the 1st Battalion who were about to sail to Korea.

Colonel the Hon. David Arbuthnott

Came to know the Queen Mother through the Black Watch, of which he became regimental secretary. The Queen Mother was Colonel-in-Chief from 1937.

The first regimental occasion I remember with the Queen Mother was when the 1st Battalion paraded before going to Korea, in the early summer of 1952, not long after King George VI died. It was a very memorable occasion, because she was in court mourning and was entirely in black, and everybody had black arm bands. There we were, parading on this former naval air station overlooking the sea – a beautiful setting, and a lovely day, windy and sunny – and she came and said goodbye to us. It's a tradition, to see every battalion before they leave for overseas service.

We like to think she has a special feeling for the Black Watch. We always think very highly of the Glamis-Angus-Black Watch connection. In the same way as when you speak to her individually, she makes you seem to be the only person that matters, collectively, when she's with the Black Watch, she has that wonderful knack of making the Black Watch seem to be the organisation that matters. Before she became Colonel-in-Chief, her brothers and cousins served in the regiment, particularly in the First World War. Glamis was a hospital during that war, and she did some nursing, and I suppose a number of Black Watch officers convalesced there. There's a third connection in that there used to be a Black Watch holiday home just outside Dundee, which Queen Elizabeth's mother was closely involved in setting up after the First World War. The idea was to have a place where widows and orphans of Black Watch soldiers could go for a holiday by the sea. It was in 1925 when Queen Elizabeth first came with her mother to this home, and she's been back about every three or four years.

There is a super atmosphere when she comes on regimental occasions. Perhaps we're being presumptuous, but wc think of it as a sort of family atmosphere. She's well-known to everybody, and knows a lot of their fathers. We get the impression that she's coming back to a place and people that she knows well. I don't think anybody presumes to become too informal. Very relaxed, without being informal, is probably the best desription. It would never be so relaxed that everybody took their jackets off and rolled their sleeves up; colonels and sergeant-majors would be furious if it was. We talk to her about regimental matters, and things like fishing, stalking and farming. On the regimental side it's a lot to do with fathers, uncles, and cousins of the individual she's speaking to. And, of course, she has the same connection with the wives and children; she will have known some of the wives' fathers in the Black Watch, and will remember them. She has a remarkable memory, and will pick you up on something that you've got wrong. She's invariably right.

I particularly remember that time she came here in 1987 to present Colours to the Territorial Army battalion based here in Perth, and there was a break in the proceedings. She came into Balhousie Castle, our headquarters, and we thought it would interest her to see photographs of the parade when she presented Colours to the predecessor of this battalion. That parade took place at Glamis about fifty years ago. We went over these photographs and had a lot of fun together, picking out the various officers, and talking about where their sons were, and how many of them were there that day, and she could certainly remember more of the faces than I could. It was remarkable. But that's my impression of her – an incredibly quick mind, a very warm personality, a lovely twinkle in the eye and that complete absorption in the person with whom she's speaking. It makes you feel terrific to be considered the most important person at the moment. These are the main characteristics that stick in my mind. I think she's smashing.

Major-General Andrew Watson

A friend of the Queen Mother's through the Black Watch, he became Colonel of the Regiment during part of her long period as Colonel-in-Chief. Also Lieutenant-Governor of the Royal Hospital, Chelsea.

We are a family regiment and are connected with the counties of Perth, Angus and Fife. One of the great families of Angus is obviously the Strathmores, and so they have always been part of the family regiment. As a member of the Strathmore family, the Queen Mother was brought up at Glamis, and her father, her brothers and uncles, cousins and so on all served in the Black Watch. I suppose when King George V died there couldn't have been a more suitable person to succeed him as Colonel-in-Chief than the Duchess of York, as she then was.

When she visits the regiment it's amazingly informal. One feels that she's coming to see her family, so to speak, and that's the way we feel about her. She has got fantastic presence, and she makes everyone completely at ease with her charm and her terrific sense of humour. She enormously enjoys being in company, and meeting people, and that enjoyment spreads to the people she meets. They are enchanted, and when she leaves at the end they realise they've been with a very special person. I am fortunate enough to see her reasonably often and she really takes a deep interest in getting up-to-date with all we've been doing. When, for instance, the regiment is abroad I write to her Private Secretary about once every six months to tell him what's been going on, and when I see her later she thanks me, and has clearly taken it all in.

We had a tremendous parade recently in Germany, celebrating her fiftieth year as Colonel-in-Chief of the Black Watch. The Jocks realised it was a very special occasion, and they're so totally devoted to their Colonel-in-Chief that they put on a parade, the like of which I have never seen before. They worked incredibly hard at it, and the Queen Mother quite clearly appreciated that, and mentioned it several times to me when we were watching it. She was almost jumping up and down in her seat with excitement. As the parade ended, instead of the normal dismissal, it was decided that the battalion should march off into the trees at the back. So there was this marvellous sight of the pipes and drums leading the whole battalion of something like five hundred and fifty Jocks away out of sight through the trees. As this was happening, I suggested to the Queen Mother that we might go and meet some of the important people who were waiting to see her, but she said: 'Certainly not. I'm going to wait till we have seen the whole battalion disappear into the trees.' And I detected a tear in her eye at that stage.

She devoted a very long time to us that day. She arrived at eleven and was with us till about half past three. I suggested to her Private Secretary, Martin Gilliat, that perhaps that should be the end of it, because it was a very tiring and hot day, but that we would love her to have dinner with us that night in the Mess. And I had the message back to say that she'd like that very much indeed. When I asked what time the car should come to take Her Majesty back, I was surprised to hear that it had been fixed for half past eleven. So that really was a very long day. But she does have amazing stamina.

Another incident which comes very much to mind was when we were having a Black Watch reunion at Kirknewton in September 1986, and we'd laid on a sort of Highland Games with tents and sideshows and pipes and drums and tossing the caber, and all that sort of business. The night before, we'd had a really bad storm, and all the tents were blown down. In the morning there was still a dreadful gale and driving rain. We were very surprised that Her Majesty's helicopter came at all from Birkhall, and I suspect it had something to do with her determination not to let us down. After lunch we went down to the games. The

Major-General Andrew Watson showing the delight which always accompanied the Queen Mother's visits to the regiment whether at home in Scotland or abroad.

tents had been put back up, but it was still incredibly bad weather, very strong wind and rain. I suggested to Her Majesty that perhaps it would be better if she went to a tent and then people could be brought to her, rather than going round all the company tents to meet all the Jocks, their wives and all the relatives. But she said: 'Certainly not. I shall continue going round.' And we went round for about two hours in really dreadful conditions, and she apparently thoroughly enjoyed it.

When she talks to the Jocks it's very animated, because they feel she is just one of them. She's an Angus girl, and I suppose nearly half the battalion come from Dundee or Angus. She'll ask them about things at home and people or things that they mutually know about. It's terribly easy, and the Jocks are never short of words in any case. She loves Jock stories. We have had quite a few giggles together over stories about the Jocks. I try and use the vernacular a bit when I tell them. She actually tells one or two rather good ones herself, but I don't think I'm going to tell you them.

When you sit next to her at dinner, it's the easiest thing in the world. She makes it so easy for you to talk about all sorts of things – her own family, our families, world affairs. Being a military man, I find she's particularly interested in knowing what the army's doing, what they feel about things and so on. She has talked to me a lot about the war and how much she got out of her visits to units and people all over the country. She particularly mentioned a visit to a squadron of Norwegian fighter pilots who, she said, were absolutely lovely.

I have been lucky enough to have one or two lunches at Clarence House. Again it's very informal – rather like going to any other person's lunch party. Obviously the surroundings are superb and when you go to the table it's absolutely groaning with silver and fruit and china, and just full of the most marvellous *objets d'art* and glass. The food is tremendous and quite a lot of it too. I particularly remember having half a chicken, which was quite delicious, but I found that I was talking so much to the Queen Mother that I still had most of it left when everyone else had finished, which was somewhat embarrassing.

I am also Lieutenant-Governor of the Royal Hospital in

Chelsea, and I can give another example of her charisma. The name of the person taking the parade on Founder's Day is always traditionally announced at Christmas Dinner the year before. I have never heard such a roar of approval from the pensioners as we had on the day it was announced that she would be taking the next parade. On Founder's Day itself many of them march, but a number of them sit on seats all around the parade ground. They're too old and they have bad legs and all that sort of thing. But on this particular occasion the seats were very much emptier than normal. They were all quite determined to show the Queen Mother that they wished to be on parade for her. They would have all been serving in the First World War at the time she was nursing the convalescents at Glamis, and I've read letters to the effect that she was just an angel administering to the wounded at that time. It all shows that she has certainly got more than just the regal side which we all respect and admire. Even before she married into the Royal Family she had those qualities of happiness and caring for others.

I feel that Queen Elizabeth is almost a part of my life. I first met her in 1946 when she visited us in Perth, and the impression has always been the same – of this gracious person who takes enormous enjoyment out of meeting her regiment or, indeed, anybody else, and who has a marvellous sense of humour and enjoyment. She really is irreplaceable in a way. She'll be a tremendous loss to us because of that quality she has, and the sort of loyalty, which transcends anything I know, which she generates in other people. I'm sure this isn't just true of the Black Watch, but of the country as a whole.

Yeoman Warder Joe Hubble

Former warrant officer in the Black Watch, though himself a Londoner. He met the Queen Mother often through her association with the regiment. After retiring from the army, he became one of the yeoman warders at the Tower.

I would often see her when I was on guard duty at Balmoral. Part of the duty is to beat over the heather each day for the royal shoots. There are numerous occasions when you go off with individual members of the Royal Family, like with the Queen Mother when she goes off to shoot woodcock and occasionally to fish. Irrespective of whether it was a fine day or a damp Scottish day the Queen Mum always came across at lunch time and enquired as to whether your food was good, and how you were all keeping during your tour of duty. She always came down to the barracks at Ballater and had, not an inspection, but a look round. She went through the cookhouse and the sleeping quarters, enquiring as to whether things were going well. I always used to believe that she was checking up to see whether jobs had been carried out or improvements from her previous year's look round. She is very acute at spotting little details and after she'd been told they were due for a change next year, she would check to see that it had been done.

There were also men selected to attend the Ghillies' Ball, which occurred twice during your ten-week period. During that evening there were many soldiers who had the great honour to dance with members of the Royal Family. I danced with the Queen Mum because the Black Watch sergeants always dance the 'Dashing White Sergeant'. She is an exceptionally good dancer, but I was extremely nervous at the time and I would have thought anybody was a good dancer.

I first saw the Queen Mother when she came to see the battalion before we went off to the Korean War. I was only a Jock in the battalion then. I believe the men in the regiment are honoured when the Queen Mother arrives. They look forward to it, and refer to it as Mum coming to visit us. Before the battalion went off to Cyprus a few years later the Queen Mother came round our quarters. She was having a look round in her usual way, and when she went into the kitchen her first comment was: 'This has been designed by a man.' She was looking up at the very thick frosted glass above the cooker and said: 'No woman would have ever designed a place like this.' Then to my horror, my young daughter, who had disappeared while I was showing the Queen Mother around, reappeared and went up to her and said: 'That's for you, lady,' and gave her the dish cloth. I stood there shocked, but the Queen Mum just shook her head, smiled and said: 'That is exactly what my own grandchildren would have done!'

In 1987 the Queen Mother celebrated fifty years as a Colonel-in-Chief of the regiment, and I had the great honour to go across to Berlin as a Yeoman of the Guard, wearing state dress which had not gone out of the country before. I was to escort the Queen Mother through the ranks of the 1st Battalion, who were stationed there. It was a wonderful day. I would say in all my twenty-eight years of service it was the finest day I had ever witnessed, and talking to the Queen Mother after, she said it was one of the finest parades she had ever seen. She added: 'I know because I have been in the regiment longer than you.' When the battalion were marching off the parade ground, over the hill to disappear down in the woods at the rear of the barracks, the colonel of the regiment, Major-General Watson, said to me: 'Be prepared to move now, Mr Hubble, we are going to take the Queen Mother across so that she can meet the representatives of the American and French forces.' So I shouldered my partisan ready to march off, but the Queen Mother said: 'Mark time, Mr Hubble. We are not going anywhere until the battalion have marched over the hill. This is a wonderful sight.' And indeed it was. I actually saw the Queen Mother, as she moved off at the end, dabbing at a tear in her eye, after watching the battalion in kilts, spats, colours flying and bayonets glinting in the sun.

Yeoman Warder
Joe Hubble (back centre)
wearing full state dress,
Berlin, 1987.

The Queen Mother went off to dine in the Officers' Mess with the thirteen remaining colonels who had served during her period of command. I myself went off to be wined and dined in the Warrant Officers' and Sergeants' Mess. Then in December we had the Regimental Association dinner of the Black Watch in London, and my wife and I were presented again to the Queen Mother. She said: 'Now that you're back, tell me what happened after I left you in Berlin.' I said: 'Late nights and sore heads.' She said: 'Excellent, excellent – as long as the battalion looked after you well.' And again she said to me what a wonderful parade and march-off it had been, and that it still stood in her mind. It is something that will last in the minds of all of us that had the honour to attend that day. It is a great saying in the Black Watch that if you put a lot into life, you get a lot from it, and I believe the Queen Mother has done this wonderfully well.

Sergeant-Major Joe Barton

Long-serving soldier in the Black Watch, which is based a few miles from Glamis Castle.

The first time I saw the Queen Mother was back in 1959, during a march we did near Balmoral. It was the 4/5th Black Watch who were actually doing the march, and I went along as one of the cadets. It was very early in the morning and the Queen Mother was standing there at the top waving to everybody as we passed. I was just a sixteen-year-old at the time. It struck me that she was out that early looking over the troops. It seemed to me that she really cared about the regiment. Since then I've met her quite frequently. I've had the honour quite a few times to be in the Guard of Honour for her, both Territorial and with the 1st Battalion. The first time was when we got the freedom of the city of Forfar, and then on numerous other occasions when she's visited the 1st Battalion. She always asks how your family is – I'm quite lucky because she actually knows my father through the Black Watch, and she mentions him now and again.

There are quite a few characters in the regiment who she knows personally. The Jocks really like her; she's very informal when she comes round, and seems to just want to talk to them and their families. She takes a great interest in everything you do, everything the regiment does, no matter where we go. The mother of our regiment – that's the best way to put it. She really cares for the Black Watch.

Sergeant Danny Donovan

Long-serving NCO in the Black Watch.

I've met the Queen Mother four times now and had a little chat – mainly since I've been in the Sergeants' Mess. She's quite informal when she comes inside. She talks about battalion life, and about our families and children. Having her as Colonel-in-Chief means a lot to everybody that serves in the regiment. She's always kept in touch; it doesn't matter whereabouts in the world we've been posted. Everybody in the Black Watch has got a lot of respect and a lot of deep feelings for the Queen Mother. She's got that kind of personality that makes you feel at home – you feel she's one of the family when you chat to her.

For Sergeant Danny Donovan the Queen Mother seemed part of the family.

Courtiers and Servants

Many of the people who held posts in the Queen Mother's Household stayed with her so long that they became her oldest friends.

The Queen Mother's birthdays, celebrated at Clarence House, gave the public a chance to see her at her London home. In the background are some of the many people who helped her run her busy life.

Lord Charteris of Amisfield

Private Secretary to Princess Elizabeth (1950–2), he was appointed Assistant Private Secretary when she became Queen, and finally Private Secretary in 1972. He retired in 1977, and became Provost of Eton the following year. An immensely popular figure of wide experience in all things royal.

I think Queen Elizabeth is fond of Eton because all her brothers were here, and she knows a great many Etonians. She loves the place, and comes here once a year for a sort of semi-official visit. It's not a great smart thing and it doesn't go in the Court Circular, but it's great fun. Sometimes she goes to chapel – the last time was when our organ was being tried out after being refurbished, and she amazed everyone by insisting on climbing into the organ loft, up a very dangerous circular stone staircase which gentlemen like me have the greatest difficulty getting up and down. However she just floated up into the loft.

Sometimes she comes in the evening when we do a performance for her – the boys sing and play, and sometimes we have a piper, and then we do little sketches. Last time she came we did a bit of P.G. Wodehouse, which she's very very fond of. We did his 'Pig-Hoo-o-o-ey', in which I played the part of Lord Emsworth. It was a huge success! Then afterwards she walks round and talks to everybody. She arrives after dinner usually – we give her a little smoked salmon or something.

I always get a list from Martin Gilliat of the boys that she wants to meet – the grandchildren of her ladies-in-waiting and that sort of thing. In a typical evening, after the performance there'll be a hundred people in the room, and she'll talk virtually to everyone. It's marvellous the way she does it – always something new to say to everybody.

I think she must have been born with a certain magic. Of course, she's thirteen years older than I am so I can't really talk about that, but my stepfather, who was about her contemporary and used to know her in the twenties, said she was absolutely fascinating. Not a classic beauty, but charm that could take the bird off the tree – and always fun. And she's also got the most marvellous manners – in the sense of making you feel at ease. I should think the young men were absolutely dotty about her. She had many people in love with her, you can bet your bottom dollar on that. But there is more to her than that. First of all, tremendous courage and absolute determination to do the thing right. At the time of the Abdication the Royal Family was given a jolly nasty knock; it wasn't good news at all. And it was King George VI and Queen Elizabeth, as they became, who picked it up and put it right where it is. Now, if you talk about the Queen anywhere in the world, you only mean the Queen of Great Britain. She played a very great part in this and was a marvellous support to the King. She was also wonderful in the war; there was no question of going away.

She has a genuine love for the arts. She's got some very good pictures which she's collected herself, and she loves the opera. She speaks beautiful French and she's highly intelligent. She really was a perfect consort. She was a marvellous wife and mother – she'd already proved that as the Duchess of York with her two children, and she just took that and put it on the world stage – the family on the throne. But she is also excellent at talking to statesmen and politicians, and perhaps laughing at some of them a little bit too, getting fun out of it. The monarchy couldn't have got through without the King being jolly good, but I think he would have had a frightful problem without a woman like that at his side. You can't measure these things, but because of her love, because of her interest and intelligence, she gave the King the confidence he perhaps lacked to begin with. He had a stutter, and it was very difficult for him. She's played a very important part constitutionally. You can't say she's saved the country, because no one person ever does that, but I would say that

Lord Charteris of Amisfield showing the Queen Mother the restored organ in College Chapel, Eton.

the King and she together saved the monarchy. That is for sure.

She has also got a great sense of humour. It's not so much wit as fun. She likes things vulgar in the sense of being 'of the people', but not coarse.

Something else she loves is Scotland. She is after all the child of a great Scottish family and she has always adored Birkhall, which she and King George VI had when they were Duke and Duchess of York. She loves Balmoral too, and she's also got the Castle of Mey, which is a fascinating place on the edge of Scotland, right up in the flat country of Caithness. She loves that because it's the only thing that is actually her own. She bought it and restored it, and as the chairman of the National Heritage Memorial Fund I'd say she did a marvellous heritage job on it. She put a roof on it and filled it with all sorts of interesting things – nothing tremendously expensive, but Caithness glass that she's bought when she's up there, and lots of blue mackintoshes hanging up and that sort of thing. She can turn anywhere into a home.

I remember staying at Balmoral in 1950, a few months after I'd joined Princess Elizabeth. It was absolutely wonderful. I was immediately conscious of Queen Elizabeth's tremendous warmth and fun. Now I quite often go to Clarence House for a meal, and to Birkhall and the Castle of Mey, and, whether it's a picnic or something grander, or simply out in the Clarence House garden under the great plane trees there, she always makes it fun. She's interested in people – there's no question of being bored in her company, or embarrassed. Instead of stiffening up, you relax.

She always produces the most marvellous food. I remember particularly, years ago when my children were young and we were all at Balmoral, she used to give the most wonderful parties at Birkhall. I remember my own children saying: 'Oh! she gives such good food!' They adored it. And there you saw a very interesting side to Queen Elizabeth. There would be a children's party with thirty or forty children, and parents and anybody who happened to be staying at Balmoral, and on many occasions I've seen Queen Elizabeth leading the conga up and down the stairs, round and back again – followed by the children, their parents and one or two cabinet ministers.

She enjoys a game of croquet at Clarence House. She plays to win, but not in the vicious way it can be played. No dirty tricks; she just likes to win like everybody does. She is also very fond of shooting, and I've had not only the honour but the extraordinary convenience of having her sometimes put my cartridges in on a grouse moor. I would describe her as the best loader in Aberdeenshire! She doesn't herself shoot, but she loves the whole thing – the hill, the heather, the lovely picnic, the keepers and the beaters. She's very much at home in that atmosphere. She is a countrywoman, but I don't think she'd be happy without London as well.

I think above all else Queen Elizabeth is absolutely authentic. She is what she always has been, the daughter of a great aristocratic house, but she's played this role on a world stage. She's absolutely the best of that type. Sometimes the kind of people I'm referring to can be very narrow in their outlook and think everybody should know his place. But she's got this extraordinary ability to get on with people, because she is very fond of them, and interested in them. This carries through, so when you're with her you feel you're the only person she's interested in for that moment, and it's a very nice feeling. It isn't just a performance, but that doesn't mean that she's not a professional. Her sense of timing is marvellous, and she will go with a sort of instinct to the person in the crowd who might perhaps have a red tie on and be a communist. She is always interested in what she does. It's a great performance, if you like, but it's an absolutely genuine one.

The Dowager Viscountess Hambleden

Daughter of the 15th Earl of Pembroke, and a lady-in-waiting to the Queen Mother for over fifty years.

I first met Queen Elizabeth when she very kindly came to my coming-out ball. She was in her early twenties, a bit older than me. I remember she looked extremely pretty – she always was particularly fascinating. I can't honestly tell you what she was wearing to the ball, in fact, I can hardly remember what I was wearing; it's a long time ago. She was a real honey-pot. Everybody was very taken with her and she had endless admirers. She was extremely natural, had a frightfully good sense of humour and was a great enjoyer of life, an enhancer if you like.

The Duke of York wanted to marry her, but I think she took some time to make up her mind because she realised the implications, not for the future, but because it would change her life. She is a very intelligent woman and was a very intelligent young lady, and she had lots of other admirers. I expect if somebody does have a lot of admirers, they have to eventually make up their mind who they like best.

I got to know the Yorks better in the thirties. They were a very popular couple to have to parties and to stay at weekends. She wasn't really in the background because whatever she did was tremendously well received. She was a popular figure with the public even before she became Queen.

When she married the Duke of York, there was no reason for her to think that she would ever be Queen, and the Abdication must have been a shock both to her and to the Duke of York. The Duke of York had been very fond of his elder brother, the

The Dowager Viscountess Hambleden (back left) in attendance on the Queen Mother's eighty-fifth birthday.

Prince of Wales. It is also much easier to succeed if your predecessor has died. The new King depended enormously on her support, but equally she never made a decision without asking him. If I asked her if she would do something, she'd always say: 'I'll just ask the King.' She relied very much on his wisdom. If he got worried or fussed or cross about anything, she would always manage, in a clever way, to turn it into a joke.

She was also a very good mother, and the children always behaved frightfully well. She would never, ever reprimand them in public, but she'd tick them off afterwards. Both the Queen and Princess Margaret are devoted to her. She understands children. There's a charming story of when she was taking Prince Charles to meet his parents. In those days they went on tours by sea, so he hadn't seen them for a long time. He was only about four or five, and as she arrived at the station she thought: 'Oh, heavens' –

and she told me this herself – 'I haven't told Charles that the regiment are going to present arms and that the noise of the guns going on to the platform will be very noisy and frightening.' But it was too late to do anything! I asked her what happened and she said: 'I was afraid he was going to cry, so all I did was to hold his hand very, very tight. I was so proud of Charles; he got crimson in the face, but he never cried.' I think that shows she was a good psychologist.

During the war she and the King went to all the towns that were bombed. They went to see the troops – the Poles in Scotland, and the American airforce in Norfolk. I was very fortunate in going to all these places on the royal train, including Liverpool when they were preparing the invasion of North Africa. That was all very exciting. It was tremendously secret and, owing to security, one didn't always see an enormous amount of people in the streets like you do now. However, word usually got around so there were often more people than were expected. I remember once we were going to Norfolk. As we were about to start there was an air raid warning, so everybody had to go downstairs, much to the annoyance of the King, who thought it was quite unnecessary. As soon as the all-clear sounded, we rushed off to the station and got into the train, where everybody had to dust themselves down, because the bombs had fallen quite near. They were both very philosophical and brave; they were going to carry on whatever happened. They were also very strict about rationing. We were always quite hungry in the train, so I used to take a packet of biscuits. There was no question of having more food; they always had exactly the same amount of sugar and pats of butter as we all had.

I've been lucky enough to travel even more with Queen Elizabeth since the war. I went to Kenya twice, and I've been to Uganda and Rhodesia, North and South – what's now called Zimbabwe – and to Canada, Italy, France, Denmark, and other countries. It's not a rest cure, but tremendously broadening and interesting. A typical day would start at about half past nine in the morning, in an aeroplane flying somewhere, and would end after several aeroplane flights with a large dinner, and probably bed at half past twelve or one. A lot of her entourage feel absolutely exhausted, but she always looks remarkably untired, despite standing for hours on end.

During visits, if necessary she will sometimes be late leaving a place because she thinks it is more important to spend ten minutes talking to somebody than to pass by altogether for the sake of sticking to the schedule. Sometimes it puts the people who are in charge in rather a tizzy, but she is quite unmoved and carries on. She is not unpunctual, not like Queen Alexandra who was known to be very unpunctual. Wherever she goes she will always see the press on the first day and ask them for drinks at Government House – we always stay at Government House, whatever the country. Talking to the press is a very good idea, as she charms them all.

She particularly liked Africa. I think she was thrilled by the countryside, and she loved the safari part of it. When she is travelling she is always very considerate. If you'd spent the morning going down a mine, which we did in Rhodesia, then lunch and then a long journey in a car, she would always say to me, or whoever was in-waiting: 'Now I am going to close my eyes for ten minutes – you keep yours open, and if there's a crowd of people just give me a nudge and I'll wave to them.' And after her rest she'd say: 'Now you can go to sleep.' All the years that I've been with her I have never known her cross, and that really is a great thing to say of somebody, because things can be irritating.

Once in Kenya we visited the Masai tribe. We left quite early in the morning, and she said: 'The Masai won't have a clue who is the Queen, because they'll have only seen pictures showing a crown, but I'll dress as near as I can to looking like that.' So she wore a wonderful hat with feathers on, and she put on The Garter in the aeroplane, which was rather alarming because it was a very small plane. We arrived and the whole crowd were totally silent. They just stood with their spears, and the young warriors were all covered with lions' heads, and had covered their faces in dung. It was very, very hot, and the smell was unbelievable. She made a speech, which was translated, and then in the middle of lunch the rain suddenly came down. It was rather like an English garden party, everything was completely sodden. We had to leave rather early in case the aeroplane couldn't get off the airstrip, but now the crowd were cheering like anything, so I said to the man who was next to me: 'Why are they so cheerful now?' And he said: 'Don't you realise we haven't had rain for three months and they're all shouting: "Long live the rain goddess!"' So she went in a cloud of glory, having brought the rain.

She's very good at getting on with people and making them feel relaxed so they are no longer shy. She has this quality of making them feel quite at home. She loves television and she can talk all about the programmes. Of the more frivolous ones, she adores *Dad's Army*, *'Allo 'Allo* and *The Two Ronnies*. She also reads a lot. She simply loves *Mapp and Lucia* and in all the bedrooms at Birkhall there's always a copy for the guests. She is very fond of P. G. Wodehouse as well. Noël Coward was a favourite; he was very good company. He played and sang at Sandringham once when I was there and everybody joined in. She likes that sort of thing.

Queen Elizabeth is a very strong character with very strong feelings. She often has to curb those feelings about, say, politics. She is tolerant of the young, but she does think there ought to be standards, and I think she is sad that some of them have fallen by the wayside. She feels manners are very important – more so than, say, clothes. She's not very interested in her own clothes and often says they are a bore. The photographs that Cecil Beaton took of her earlier on were frightfully good and he was quite instrumental in her adopting the type of clothes she still wears, chiffons and so on, because they obviously suited her.

My feelings for Queen Elizabeth are of deep affection and tremendous admiration. She is enormously sympathetic, very kind and wonderfully good to all the staff. They simply love her. Whenever she gets out of the car, even when she's only been out for half an hour she always says 'thank you' to the chauffeur. A lot of people don't do that, if they are lucky enough to have a chauffeur. She has a wonderful nature.

Lady Jean Rankin

Daughter of the 12th Earl of Stair, she joined the Queen Mother, then Queen, as Woman of the Bedchamber in 1947

It was a great privilege and a great surprise when somebody asked me to think about being a lady-in-waiting. I had only met Queen Elizabeth a couple of times before. I think they must have been hard up; they couldn't think of anybody. I was skiing in Switzerland when I had a letter saying somebody had suggested I might make a lady-in-waiting, and what did I think about it. Could I give any reason why I shouldn't? So I wrote back saying I was sorry, but I hadn't got a big enough piece of paper to give all the reasons. But anyway, I started in 1947 and have loved it ever since. One meets such interesting people and there is so much variety; one has stayed at the White House with Eisenhower and so on. There's a lot of ordinary office work as well. We do a fortnight on duty at a time. It may be in London or Sandringham, or it may be in Scotland. At Clarence House we just have an ordinary sort of office morning. She probably rings for you in the course of the morning, and you go through with a basket full of letters and discuss those you have got that you need an answer for. Then she gives you others that she wants written. It's more informal at Birkhall. Her Majesty goes out every morning with the dogs, regardless of the weather, probably at about half past ten in the morning. After which she either sends for one or comes into the office, which is just next door to her sitting room.

Part of one's job is to look after house guests, find out what they want, take them shopping in Ballater and so on. She has an immense number of friends and she remembers everybody in a marvellous way. It is rather sad in a way, because our own generation is obviously greatly diminished.

She loves young people and is a wonderful hostess. Evenings are great fun – you are quite liable to end up dancing in the drawing room. She has got the most wonderful sense of humour. Sometimes at a party she will disappear and in will come the most extraordinary figure, dressed in weird clothes, including a bowler hat and walking stick. Often people don't realise at first that it is Queen Elizabeth. She likes burlesque and dressing up and that kind of thing. We used to play The Game a lot, which involves mini-acting. She is also extremely fond of cards, and is very good at things like Canasta and Racing Demon. And in any brief interval before someone arrives, out comes the card table and she'll have a game of patience.

She loves gardening too, wherever she is. The garden at Royal Lodge is beautiful. The King was a very good gardener, deeply interested, and he more or less created that garden. He was still alive when I started in 1947, but he only had five years to live. It was a very worrying time for Queen Elizabeth because he was often ill, although it was always concealed as much as possible. He was a delightful and charming person, and was very brave about his difficulties.

The King's death was a terrible thing for her. I was with her a great deal, and she didn't see people for a long, long time. He died in February, and in July or August, when she was up in Scotland, somebody rang me from Balmoral and said Winston Churchill was there and wanted to know how she was and if she was seeing anybody yet. I said: 'Don't ask – tell him to come over.' So he came without asking if he should, and she saw him, and from then on she started to see people again. I think he must have said things which made her realise how important it was for her to carry on, how much people wanted her to do things as she had before.

That was also the time when she first saw the Castle of Mey. She has a great friend who had a house called The House of the Northern Gate, up in Caithness. She went to stay up there, and I went with her. It was the first place she had been to where there weren't associations with the King, and she gained a sort of relaxation and peace from it. Then, when we were driving around, she saw this house and was told it was quite interesting. When she went to see it the owner said he was going to take the roof off, and she said: 'Oh, no! You can't do that, it's much too beautiful.' Shortly afterwards she decided she would like to buy it. It was bought for a trivial sum, but quite a lot had to be done to it because it was rather primitive. It is very nice inside, though I haven't been there for years. It's not on my beat as it were – I always go to Birkhall. Lady Fermoy goes up to the Castle of Mey. Queen Elizabeth has got a special soft spot for it. She says: 'This is the only one that belongs to me.'

Since I joined, I've travelled thousands of miles with her, including going round the world completely. It's very tiring, you start your day possibly at three or four in the morning, and go to bed at one o'clock the next morning, though it's not always as bad as that. She keeps going because she's got very good stamina. She never seems tired, even though it must be so much harder for her than for other people. She is on view and being talked to all the time, whereas other people can opt out, turn away, forget.

Queen Elizabeth has very strong views on how things should be done. She has a gentle exterior, but there is great strength underneath it. Steel. I have very rarely seen her angry, but I have once or twice.

She rises above difficulties – after all, she has been confronted with some terrible things. She minded the Abdication terribly, because she felt that it did so much damage to the King, and shortened his life. He was the last person who wanted to take on that very heavy task. He was a very shy person, so it was a tremendous effort for him to make speeches; public occasions were a trial to him. When he was younger he stammered quite badly, but by the time I knew him, you hardly ever heard it. Occasionally, if something annoyed him intensely, there was a little hesitation. Queen Elizabeth's support at the time of the Abdication showed the world that there was strength and purpose, and a strong family on the throne, with a new atmosphere. The previous members of the Royal Family didn't have great charm, though they were nice enough people. When she came into the family, and had two daughters who were attractive and pretty, it made a difference from the previous generation, who were very buttoned-up and not at all relaxed. She has had an enormous influence on the popularity of the monarchy today. One looks back on the Abdication and the general rage and the dislike of Mrs Simpson, but in the end we came out of it extremely well. King George VI made such an admirable King and Queen Elizabeth such a marvellous consort, so I often feel that Mrs Simpson ought to be thanked, rather than reviled.

Charles Oulton

Later to become steward (senior servant) at Buckingham Palace, he was a footman there at the time of the Queen Mother's wedding in 1923.

It was at Sandringham that I first saw her just after her engagement to the Duke of York, in the early 1920s. I thought how different she was from the sort of people we had seen before – European princesses and so on had been the norm during George V's time. She was a very vivacious young woman. Ordinary, if you like, quite ordinary, and obviously very popular with George V. There was never any doubt about whether George V liked you or not. She was very talkative, and I suppose he liked that, and nice to look at too – very attractive. She spoke to us as she would speak to anybody else, no difference at all. She wasn't full of airs and graces.

Working at the Palace I saw more of her when she became Queen. She didn't change at all. She has always been the sort of person that we see now. I went with them to Canada in 1939. It was a very important visit, judging by the enormous crowds, and the reception they had. They were very popular wherever they went. They crossed Canada twice, once on the Canadian Pacific Railway, and then on the Canadian National on the way back. They went to America too, where they were met at the station in Washington by the President and his wife. That really was an occasion.

Later on during the war we used to travel by train with them. Journeys from London usually started from either Euston or King's Cross, according to which part of the country they were visiting. They used the royal train with two special coaches – one for the King and one for the Queen, each with their sitting room, bedroom, bathroom and so on. Often we were going to a place that had been bombed, probably a few days previously, so something would be arranged very quickly. When we got there I remained on the train, so I only saw the crowds at the station to greet them.

She loves meeting people. She has a way with them. I think it is her friendly approach, and her smile; she disarms people. There are one or two others in the Royal family who are very approachable and friendly, and, I suppose, very popular. Princess Alexandra, for instance, is a very talkative young woman and a very friendly person, but I don't think anyone supersedes the Queen Mother. She can be a little late now and then. I think she starts off punctually but ends up being very late, simply because she has so much to say to people and no one is left out. When she was there the atmosphere at the Palace was very happy. The present Queen has said to me that Buckingham Palace does not lend itself to happiness. Those were her own words and she is certainly right. Yet in King George and Queen Elizabeth's reign it was a place where one felt at ease and happy. In general, any house that she lived in was a happy house. I saw much more of them at Balmoral and Sandringham. They were smaller houses and there was a different way of going on altogether, domestic and very easy and relaxed. I wouldn't describe the Palace as a home at all. Queen Elizabeth preferred Sandringham and Balmoral, especially Balmoral, because she was in Scotland. She was quite happy anywhere, but happiest, I am sure, at Balmoral.

One personal thing about her I remember was at the time my father died. I was on my way to Sandringham. I arrived there and had to leave the following day. Queen Elizabeth was part of the party at Sandringham on that occasion. I should think about two months later I was at their private door when she was arriving at Buckingham Palace, and she said how sorry she was to hear that my father had died. I was quite taken back, because I can't understand how she could possibly have remembered it after all that time. I was very pleased indeed.

Group Captain Peter Townsend

Equerry to King George VI (1944–52). Comptroller of the Queen Mother's Household after the King's death, until his romantic attachment to Princess Margaret was brought to an end because of his previous divorce. Afterwards lived abroad.

Very early on in my time as an equerry, at Easter in 1944, the King and Queen and their two daughters went to Sandringham. The big house at Sandringham was shut during the war and there was another much smaller house called Appleton Lodge, I think. The lady-in-waiting and myself were in this house with the Royal Family, and so one was very close to them indeed. I'd stepped almost out of the cockpit into the home of the Royal Family, and they were simply sweet. They couldn't have been more natural and kind or made things easier. It was the same in London. Sometimes they'd say: 'Come in and have tea,' or perhaps it would be dinner.

I remember once when dinner was over we were having coffee and there was the most enormous explosion. Everybody rose about a foot in the air and sank back again, but the King and Queen were very phlegmatic. The King told me to go and find out what had happened. In fact it was that terrible V2 which fell on a pub very close to Selfridges, and killed hundreds of people. I remember another occasion when they went to visit an anti-aircraft battery, and the V1s were coming over. I was praying that the guns would never hit one, because if they just hit the tail, it might come down and explode at our feet. But there again they were both extremely phlegmatic. They refused to leave Buckingham Palace. Many of us know that they were nearly killed by a bomb which fell a few yards from them in the inner courtyard. I stood close to the King during investitures with flying bombs going past the windows, longing myself to go underground somewhere.

As a royal couple they were really an example to their people. The King relied on her very much, and had done from the beginning. We all know that he had an impediment in his speech, which in private company one never noticed. He was a very lovable man, but shy. The stammer would come out in a set speech, and there were some words he would find difficult to say.

I remember as a very small boy being in the middle of the front rank at Haileybury, where I was at school, when they came on a visit. They were Duke and Duchess of York then, and I got a very close up view of the Duke and his most impressive naval uniform, frock coat and so on. Even as a small boy one realised that he found it hard to get some words out, and I still have this impression of the Duchess of York just sending out these waves of sympathy and support. It was obvious that he admired her tremendously. Later, when I was working for them, I noticed her tremendous stamina. Those long day visits were extremely tiring, but she very seldom showed it. She was indefatigable, and always had this way of putting people at their ease, talking to them as if they weren't strangers.

At Balmoral she loved going up on the hill – to the hill, I think the Highlanders say – and would be dressed in such a way that nobody would realise she was the Queen. She would go walking down the road with her friends or her daughters, and you could see the vitality. Then in the evening there was a happy family party maybe, with quite a lot of guests, and sometimes charades afterwards, and she would always be the heart and soul of the party. They were the most marvellous family. The King and Queen were wonderful parents. They were both loved by their daughters, and vice versa. There was a wonderful balance in that family; there was a tremendous lot of fun and teasing, but there was an invisible discipline. They behaved to one another in such a way as to keep the balance going. It was a really top family.

Queen Elizabeth is a very – I was nearly going to say funny lady, but she is somebody who adores fun, and everybody has

Group Captain Peter Townsend as the King's equerry, following the opening of the South African Parliament in 1947.

fun when they are with her. Some of the laughs we had were just tremendous. I can recall playing Canasta – I'm not a card player at all, but somehow I learnt this dreadful game – and the laughs we had in the evening at Sandringham. I can't think today, some thirty or thirty-five years later, why Canasta was such a funny game, but the Queen and Princess Margaret and Princess Elizabeth made it funny. We had tremendous laughs about many other things as well. Maybe doing a little post-mortem after a big 'do', or mimicking the way someone would talk, not unkindly, but they liked to see the comic side of life. Queen Elizabeth could be firm too, but it would hardly be seen. She had the most wonderful blue eyes, and that encouraging and reassuring smile. If she was angry, she would keep the smile going, sometimes with a little difficulty, but the eyes would gleam and that was enough –

anyway it was enough for me! I presume it was enough for the daughters as well.

When the King died it was terrible. Everybody felt it deeply, but she, being so close to him, was shattered. Yet she bore her sorrow and her grief with amazing courage and fortitude. Then, of course, she had to find a new way of life. But I think that with her intelligence and her queenly *métier*, as the French call it, the new role came naturally to her. She was well capable of getting on top of the new job, and as we've all seen, she performs her role as Queen Mother in the most warm and queenly way. At the time of the relationship between Princess Margaret and myself she was wonderful all the way through, and most sympathetic. She was extremely concerned and worried, how could she be otherwise? It was a very difficult situation for her and her family. I have seen her on occasions since. I remember when there was a reunion of HMS *Vanguard*, the battleship in which the Royal Family sailed to South Africa in 1947 for the royal tour. The tour lasted three months, including, I think, thirty-six nights sleeping in a train, or trying to sleep, and it was a very rigorous experience for the Royal Family. Well, at the reunion I was waiting to meet the Queen Mother, having not seen her for years. A little before she got to me, I think she sighted me there, and to my great surprise, and I must say pleasure, she made a little sign. I hope not too many people saw it, but it was the sign one used to make when dancing the 'Boogie-woogie', which was an old, funny dance we used to do. I'm not much of a dancer myself, but the Royal Family enjoyed these dances – the Lambeth Walk, the Boogie-woogie, I Came, I Saw, I Conquered. They all joined in with tremendous spirit and verve. I also had the very great honour of being invited to the Queen Mother's eightieth-birthday garden party.

I would say she is one of the most wonderful ladies that I've ever met in my life. Not least because she is the mother of the present Queen, but also because she is full of fun, very human, and has such a simplicity and a readiness to give affection to strangers.

Major Thomas Harvey

The Queen Mother's Private Secretary during her later years as Queen (1946–51). His wife, Lady Mary, was Woman of the Bedchamber to the Queen Mother (1961–63).

It was a very interesting period when I started with Queen Elizabeth. Things were getting going after the war; there was a new government, a change from Winston Churchill, and a lot of young untried ministers. The Queen was also keen for the Princesses to widen their spheres of activity, especially Princess Elizabeth. As a result, I took her to the Juvenile Courts, the London Fire Brigade, Battersea Power Station, and all sorts of different places. It was a very happy period for the Queen Mother – the Queen as she was then – because she had two attractive daughters growing up, and there were young men, parties and dancing. They were a little restricted in their ability to entertain by the rationing which everybody else was suffering from, but there was still a terrific sense of freedom after the strains of the war. The children could get round the country and see the people, so it was a happy time in that way.

I was the Queen's Private Secretary for five years or so. The bulk of the fan-mail correspondence was handled by the ladies-in-waiting, and my jobs were really to do with the functions which the Queen attended and all her visits. Naturally anything she did with the King was organised by the King's Secretary, and so it was really her solo work that I was concerned with. It might involve her regiments, charities of various kinds, visiting hospitals, or touring cities. As it was fairly soon after the end of the war, there were a lot of places she wanted to revisit. The reception she got was always very warm and friendly. She liked to keep the visit as informal as possible, but naturally if you're

Major Thomas Harvey remained a friend long after he ceased to be the Queen Mother's Private Secretary.

visiting a city, your host is the mayor or lord mayor, and those occasions tend to fall into a fairly stereotyped pattern. A lunch in one Town Hall is very similar to lunch in any other Town Hall, but she gave a special touch of her own personality to those occasions; you never got the slightest hint of *déjà vu*. She had this ability to express interest and surprise at something which probably wasn't very surprising at all. When people are due to be introduced to Queen Elizabeth they feel rather nervous beforehand, but they always emerge very much more relaxed than they go in. Of course, one of the duties of the members of the

Household is to try to relax people, rather than to fill them with foreboding, and we did try, but nothing to the extent that she was able to. People came away from meeting her on cloud nine.

Many of the King's activities were undertaken on the advice of ministers, but this wasn't the case with the Queen. She could, obviously within reason, do what she liked as far as planning visits went, but they did most of the big ones together. She had her interests, in London and Dundee universities, and in essentially feminine things like needlework and gardens and things of that sort. She was interested in the London Garden Society, and seeing how people manage to make attractive gardens in rather unpromising circumstances. Of course, she has enjoyed her own gardens very much.

She loved the relaxation of the evening after a day which many people would have felt was full enough – even to the extent of dancing reels on some occasions. The King and Queen enjoyed charades too, and always had fun after dinner at Windsor during the Easter break, when members of the government used to come and stay for the night, and still do, I think. They enjoyed playing silly games, such as passing a match box from one nose to the other. It was quite amusing to see Queen Mary and Sir Stafford Cripps exchanging match boxes, nose-tip to nose-tip.

I never met a better hostess or one more likely to give her guests all the fun in the world. I think the secret is her thoughtfulness, the comfort of her homes, and the very nice staff of servants she has always had, quite apart from her Household. The moment a guest arrives, he or she's immediately relaxed and is made to feel at home. A lot of consideration goes into choosing what might entertain a particular group, and a plan might be made as to what to go to see. Perhaps some pictures somewhere, or a garden somewhere else, or a ruin, according to how they might feel.

On the more serious side, the Cumberland Lodge scheme owes a lot to her. It was an idea in which the King and the Queen were both involved from the very beginning, to lend Cumberland Lodge, a very precious house in Windsor Park, to a college to inculcate Christian values. Not with a view to evangelising, but to show that the Christian concept of a person's job went beyond its purely technical aspects, and to encourage students to look beyond the business of simply passing exams. Thanks to her it's now in a very flourishing condition.

I will remember Queen Elizabeth as someone who was always a pleasure to see and talk to, either about serious or light-hearted things. One always came away with a new angle on things, always aware that she wasn't going to be pushed into doing something in a hurry, or against her instincts, without a good deal of thinking first. I think her instincts are very well developed and that she has a feeling for what is suitable for her, and what is right, for what should be pursued and what is irrelevant.

Lieutenant-Colonel Sir Martin Gilliat

The Queen Mother's Private Secretary from 1956–1993. The most approachable of courtiers, Sir Martin was her right-hand man during most of her period as Queen Mother.

I came in 1955, three years after the King's death. By that time Queen Elizabeth hadn't buried the past, but she'd decided that the past was behind her, and it was necessary to start making a life of her own. It must have been an extraordinarily poignant and difficult thing to do, because she and the King did and discussed everything together. It's also quite a difficult thing to be Queen Mother, with a very young Queen who is just taking over the reins of office. One has certainly noticed that the Queen Mother has, right from the start, meticulously avoided getting involved in the Queen's affairs, except when the Queen is abroad, when as a Councillor of State she has certain duties thrust upon her. I think she made up her mind that she must – and would – forge out a way of life of her own. It has developed from that until she has turned into the best-loved grandmother, and the most attractive young person in the world; she's ageless to everybody. She's just as much loved by the young men in the Irish Guards or her regiments, as she is by contemporaries.

We have a daily routine at Clarence House. I normally open the mail, sort it out, and prepare anything special to take into Queen Elizabeth on that particular morning. Usually between half past ten and eleven, she blows for me; in other words her page, who is sort of superior footman, comes on the intercom telephone and asks me to go in. So in I go, taking a tray with everything which has come in in the last twenty-four hours, and drafts for any speeches which are coming along in the near future. She's very meticulous not to let anything go which she doesn't approve of. Quite frequently speeches which I've drafted, hopefully with great care and attention, don't get the approval, and back I go and have another try. Equally she likes to see, or be told about, every letter of any purport which comes in. The ones that the ladies-in-waiting deal with are very much more the 'ladies' fan-mail' type; endless wonderful people from all over the country wanting to know the Queen Mother's favourite recipe, and details about clothes or children or babies.

In addition to that, in the course of the morning Queen Elizabeth is very likely to see the chef, and there's a discussion about who's going to be in for what meals, and where there's going to be a luncheon or a dinner party or a picnic. Then probably on one or two days a week any one of the following might come in: the dressmaker, who traditionally has been the Norman Hartnell establishment; the hat lady or gentleman, who can spend any amount of time making sure those glorious hats, which Queen Elizabeth always wears and looks wonderful in, are right; the shoemaker, who is Mr Edward Rayne from Bond Street – a wonderful man – or any number of such people. That takes up a lot of time, probably until it's either time to go out to lunch or have lunch. Choosing between the invitations is frightfully difficult, but she's got an extraordinary instinct as to the most suitable ones, which can conveniently be fitted into her diary. She certainly is not what you would, in a theatrical sense, call typecast about things. There may be some parts of the country she goes to more often than to others, and it is conceivable that she would rather go to a botanical gardens in Birmingham than somewhere which does not interest her so much. But the other day we went up to Birmingham and she combined a morning and luncheon in the Botanical Gardens, which are the best in England after Kew, and the afternoon spent at what might be the final reunion of the Women's Land Army. Those wonderful ladies, who'd come from all parts of the British Isles, flocked into Birmingham – the Queen Mother had been frightfully good and keen about them in the war.

She also does a lot in the East End. She adores things like the

Jewish Settlements there, because she has always had a great affinity with that part of London since wartime days. Last year was a year for hospices. We did two or three by chance – there's no clear pattern. All her visits involve a great deal of travelling. She's a very meticulous traveller. Whether wc go by train, air, motorcar or sea, I've noticed that, unlike the majority of ladies in one's life, Queen Elizabeth is absolutely meticulous about the map and about where we are and how we're going. She's very accurate on points of the compass and whether we're now turning westward and that type of thing. I think that may possibly be a follow-on from being married to the King who, being a naval officer, was like that too. She finds both flying in a fixed-wing aeroplane and a helicopter absolutely second nature. Some years ago one of the Queen's Flight helicopters crashed. The Captain of the Queen's Flight was killed and we all felt great sorrow. But the Queen Mother was off in a helicopter four days afterwards – it was the same type of helicopter on the same type of journey. She's totally without nerves about any of those things.

Over the year her travels and activities do have a sort of pattern. The year starts with all the family gathered at Sandringham, and she stays there until nearly the end of January. Meanwhile I'm working in Clarence House, sending one or two huge envelopes, what's called my 'bag', each day. Then during February and March, until Easter, she's based in London through the week, with weekends almost always at Royal Lodge. That's the time of some of the great race meetings, which she's involved in, like the Grand Military meeting at Sandown, or the National Hunt meeting at Cheltenham. She doesn't go to the Grand National very much. People ask if it is because of the Devon Loch affair all those years ago, but I don't think it is; I think it just doesn't tremendously appeal to Queen Elizabeth. At Easter she joins up with the Queen at Windsor Castle, always for about ten days. Then we come back and April runs on into May. Engagements are either based in London or sometimes involve getting away for a day or more by train. Normally in about the middle of May Queen Elizabeth goes up to Birkhall on Deeside. She has people to stay with her because, if things have gone well, it's about the best salmon-fishing time of the year.

Lieutenant-Colonel Sir Martin Gilliat.

She has a lot of people staying. Though it's thought that she is a very enthusiastic fisherman herself, that isn't actually the case so much now. I think she was brilliant, but now she really prefers to encourage, watch and help others, rather than be involved in wading and fishing herself. If all goes well, most of each day in May is spent out beside the river or having picnics or wandering around. In the latter part of May she's back in London until the end of July, with engagements every day of the week, interspersed with things like the Derby, Royal Ascot and quite a lot of expeditions a fair distance away. The diary remains very full until the end of July, though we try – not always succeeding – to keep Saturdays and Sundays reasonably free. The last few days of July and the first two or three days of August are spent at Sandringham, where she's rather involved in the King's Lynn Festival, and in the various flower shows which are a sort of tradition. Then it's back here for her birthday on August the 4th, which is a terrific occasion and very traditional, with all members of the Royal Family who happen to be in London coming to lunch with the Queen Mother, hopefully in the garden under those great plane trees. The Guards march past her window with the band playing 'Happy Birthday To You'. That's always a very emotional thing. Very often in the evening there's a private visit to a theatre, a good musical if there's one going, like *Me and My Girl* or *Forty-*

Second Street, or a good straight play. Usually, on the next day or the day after, she goes to the Castle of Mey by air. The Castle isn't very large, but it's always absolutely chock-a-block with mostly young friends, who enthusiastically, or not so enthusiastically, flog out over the peat bogs to try and eliminate a rather minute proportion of the population of grouse. The Queen Mother always goes out, not actually walking with the guns, but joins them at luncheon every day for a picnic lunch.

At the end of August it's southwards as far as Aberdeenshire, to stay a few days at Balmoral, and then on to Birkhall, with a lot of Scottish engagements being done from there. There are frequent engagements in Glasgow, and a lot in Aberdeen and Dundee, done by aeroplane, car or train, starting out from Birkhall. Come the second week of October and it's back to London and Clarence House with lots of groans. Then the winter regime goes on until Christmas with the normal London engagements.

She has tremendous energy. I've now been with Queen Elizabeth since 1955 and on the whole I notice almost no difference in her vitality or her enthusiasm, and her judgement remains exactly the same. She has the most extraordinary capacity for never outwardly showing tiredness. We in the Household are all amazed that she never appears to want to have a jolly good yawn. She very rarely puts her feet up and has a sleep during the day, which all of us love to do if we can. I think that constitutionally she's wonderfully strong, and has a great ability not to worry unnecessarily; what must be, must be. Although Queen Elizabeth is in some ways a great perfectionist, she's not a fusspot, and I think that prevents her from getting unduly tired. If one's fussing like mad one gets very tired. She's a great disregarder of pain or discomfort. She would have to have a totally smashed leg or something of that sort ever to give way to it. When we say: 'Oh, you can't do that, and you must lie up,' she ignores it. The few times she has been ill in hospital and had operations, she always jumps ahead of the doctors in getting going again. Her belief in doctors is slightly tenuous. In medicine she tends towards homoeopathy rather than the more normal doctor. She's very good with doctors, and reluctantly does what they say, but basically believes that health comes from inside, and it's up to oneself to keep healthy and go on. I think that her good health helps to enable her to have such zest for life all the time.

She has a tremendous capacity for friendship. She likes outgoing people; people who've got a sense of humour, can laugh at themselves, and can be jokey. She tends to find people who are sunk into themselves less easy to become good friends with. A large number of people, when they're with Queen Elizabeth over the years, develop the technique. Obviously they like pleasing her, and she enjoys being with them; it's two-way traffic. She adores jokes and enjoys a good story. She is very competent at telling a good story in quite a few different dialects herself, with great humour and verve. It doesn't happen so much now, but when games used to be played like charades, or The Game, she was absolutely brilliant and a very good mimic and raconteur. As regards her taste in comedy, she loved the Crazy Gang. Flanagan was a personal friend of hers, and she always loved to see him and the others. It was quite low humour; they were pretty lavatorial, but that's fine, provided it's funny as well. She likes good music-hall stuff, and loves joining in and singing the choruses. She's also got a very modern side and enjoys quite a lot of modern music, plays, art and performances. I've heard her say her favourite television programme is *Dad's Army*, and then *Yes, Minister*, to which she's devoted. She adored *All Gas and Gaiters*. And she loves *The Two Ronnies*. She's a conservative enjoyer of television. She also reads a lot – biographies, autobiographies and a lot of light things. She's a tremendous P.G. Wodehouse fan. The other day she went to unveil a plaque above the house where he used to live in London. She likes E.F. Benson, and the best of Dickens and Thackeray. I don't say that she's a tremendous one for modern novels. I think she often thinks they're rather trashy, although she wouldn't say so.

She makes her own entertainment. I list them not in order of favouritism, but in the frequency with which we do them: dancing, sing-songs, reels, sometimes congas round the house, and a bit of dressing up. In daylight hours her favourite form of entertainment is walking the dogs. She loves entertaining. Any meal at which she's the hostess is always an event in itself. Everything is worked out with meticulous care and even so-called picnics can turn into exciting meals, with perhaps tables and chairs and lots of lovely pies and salads, and a lot of 'ooh, aah,' from all of the guests. She just nibbles a tiny bit herself, but she loves seeing other people enjoying it. If there's somebody who is known to be keen about a thing like bread-and-butter pudding or treacle pudding or spotted dick, she will suddenly produce that in the winter. She takes great trouble. The table always looks marvellous, with flowers galore, and the footmen in their scarlet look wonderful. That has very much gone out now. I don't think the Queen has it, but the Queen Mother does. Apparently the footmen don't mind; they do it with great distinction, and they're so proud of it.

More seriously, she has been very important to the monarchy. She has been the most superb link between all the ages of members of the Royal Family. She's been a catalyst for them all and has kept them happy and interested, by her wisdom and advice and understanding, and her sense of humour. Wherever she is one sees that, from little tiny toddlers through to those who are the same age as she is, everyone is drawn to her like a magnet. She seems to have the same effect on people at large. She gets letters from all parts of the country, and indeed the world, saying that the very effect of her being around has made them happier and has lightened their load. It's an indefinable thing. She hasn't cracked the atom or invented a wonderful aeroplane, it's just the fact of being herself.

I will always think of her as a person of such personality and vivacity, and of every day being a new adventure. She has maintained extraordinary high standards all through every phase of her life, in whatever she does. It's like being in the army; nothing but the best by her standards would ever do, and she expects the best from other people too. All that is allied with zest, sense of humour, and sense of fun. I get much joy from the fact that she's a great traditionalist. I've probably been to church with her more Sundays in my life than with anybody else. She loves traditional hymns and chants and psalms, and that is something I shall remember very much from my life with Queen Elizabeth.

Captain Sir Alastair Aird

Worked for the Queen Mother from 1960. Comptroller of her Household from 1974.

Normally about half past eleven or twelve I am summoned by the Queen Mother into her sitting room, and we then discuss anything affecting the house, or members of the staff that she is interested in. If any are getting engaged or married or are sadly leaving, we discuss either replacements or any problems affecting their lives. If there are lunch parties or other entertainments, those are all discussed, and if there are any engagements which I am responsible for, we go through those. There is always a lot of discussion about the Queen Mother's art collection – pictures going on exhibition throughout the year, and porcelain too.

I am the new boy in the Household and I have been here since 1960. My colleagues have been here longer than I have. There is always a great turnover of young staff in the kitchen, or young footmen, but the older members of staff have been with us a long time and she likes that. The staff are very loyal and devoted to her. They have always expressed to me what a wonderful person she is, and how they enjoy serving her, and if there is any hiccup in their lives, they have always said their loyalty and devotion to Queen Elizabeth comes first. The main bulk of the staff are at Clarence House, with a small number of people at Royal Lodge, Windsor. The houses in Scotland are only staffed by a housekeeper and the gardening staff. We bring all the rest up from London; chefs, stewards and so on. It's quite an administrative problem, though you always overcome it. Everyone has done the job for a number of years and they know the routine well, so we manage to get them up by rail or road or sometimes by air. It's all more relaxed in Scotland. She always gets up and takes the dogs for a walk after breakfast, comes back and has a cup of tea, and then I knock on the door with the papers which need discussion. It's more casual in other ways too. In the early days one always put a suit on for tea. Now I think one is lucky if one has got a coat on for tea. One wears much more informal clothes than one used to. I think it is a trend that has reached her via her grandchildren and other young people, who seldom have a coat these days in the country.

One of my areas of responsibility concerns her position as Admiral and Lord Warden of the Cinque Ports. These days it is purely ceremonial. In the old days the Lord Warden was an extremely important person in the land because he – it was never she before the Queen Mother – controlled the whole of the South-East part of England. The Cinque Ports produced ships and soldiers for the king, and in return they were given certain tax reliefs and a bit of local self-government. Nowadays the Queen Mother has a residence at Walmer Castle, and she is also Constable of Dover Castle, which is her headquarters. As Lord Warden she is responsible for burying any whales which are washed up on the coast of East Sussex and Kent and she gets the income from any unclaimed wrecks. So far we have buried two whales and there have been no unclaimed wrecks, so we are a bit out of pocket.

Queen Elizabeth has made a tremendous impression on me over the years. I think she is one of the most remarkable ladies I have ever met. She has a core of steel inside her. I have never really known her to lose her temper, and heavens! we have probably been aggravating enough to her. But she has got very steely blue eyes, and if you put a foot wrong, you will know it. That, I think, has been a very strong part of her character. She has always held strong convictions and believes very deeply in her religion. She can be a very compassionate and kind person, and has been very generous to many of us in various ways. She has remarkable stamina too. I have been on tours abroad with her, and we seldom get to bed until the early hours. During weekends in the country, in Scotland or down at Windsor, it's the Household that are on their knees in the early hours of the morning, while Her Majesty is still full of life. I think the main

Captain Sir Alastair Aird was with the Queen Mother from 1960. By the 1990s he was still the new boy!

reason is her constitution, and her very active brain, which is always kept busy because there are people talking to her the whole time. Being with people and travelling have been her life. Since she was eighty she has been to Canada on a couple of occasions, and this year [1988] we were down in Southern Italy and Sicily, which was extremely hot at the end of June. Rolls Royce kindly produced a car for her to travel in in Sicily, which was air conditioned, but like ladies of her age, she didn't really understand air conditioning in motor cars, and she felt she had to have all the windows open so that people could see her. That, of course, made it very hot, but she sailed through it as usual. I think that one will remember her for her kindness, her strength, and her awareness of everything that goes on. She knows something about everything in the country, whether it be architecture, politics, industry, hospital life, music or the countryside.

Tom Ewen

As ghillie for the Queen Mother during her visits to Birkhall near Balmoral, he attended her whenever she went fishing. His wife was her housekeeper.

These days Queen Elizabeth only fishes in the afternoon or the evening. She comes to me at lunchtime and says she would like to go out fishing. I arrange things and go back to the house and get the rods and everything ready. Sometimes she chooses the spot, and sometimes I say which one would be easiest and the best fish for the type of day and weather and the state of the river. There are some pools that fish better in low water and some that fish better in higher water – it just depends on the height of the water and she will always take advice on that. She always has her waders on before she comes out of the house. I just meet her at the front door, along with the chauffeur, and her policeman is always around somewhere, but you never see him. When we get to the river we just wade out and I stand there with her. She is a very good fisherman. I'd like to see all the fishermen the same as her. She's good at playing a fish, no problem with that. She chats most of the time, but she's still concentrating on her fishing. Mostly she talks about local matters and things to do with nature and the river, and fishing, of course. What I think she really likes is to be out in the open air, to be on the river, and I think a fish is a bonus to her if she gets one. Some time ago she used to stay out quite late. She even used to fish at night after dinner. Sometimes it's a better time, just when the light is changing, but she's getting older now, though you'd never know the age she is. She walks most days with the two corgis, along the river bank, and down the other side to meet the Land-Rover, which is anything up to two miles.

She has her own rod which she is very attached to. It's a twelve-foot sharp-spliced rod and she uses it all the time. There are still three or four fishing rods at the house belonging to the King, and she won't part with them, although nobody uses them. There are also two or three rifles that the King used that are still on the fire-arms certificate. She won't part with them. Sentimental value, that's what it is.

Tom Ewen and the Queen Mother await the Land Rover at the end of a day's fishing.

Mrs Sadie Ewen

Housekeeper for the Queen Mother at Birkhall, her home near Balmoral. Mrs Ewen's husband was the Queen Mother's ghillie.

When Queen Elizabeth is here, I pick up some of the staff – we have five dailies – at about quarter past five in the morning, then come into work at about half past five and do all the main public rooms. The public rooms have got to be ready before the guests come down in the morning, so they are done from about half past five to eight o'clock. I just say good morning to my husband Tom, who is a ghillie, when he comes in at eight. Then I work on until about two o'clock, and go home until five. I come back at five, and go home again at about ten in the evening when Queen Elizabeth has gone in for dinner, and the guests have got everything they want. It's a long day, but it's only when Queen Elizabeth is in residence. I have got to be here in case they need anything or in case someone's ill, because I have got all the doctors' numbers and things like that. Last year we had ninety-one people from April to the end of October, so it is a busy house, and sometimes you wonder where you are going to put them all. But usually Queen Elizabeth can shift them around from here to there, and push somebody from one room to another to make room for somebody else. She is marvellous, really. When I first came there used to be five people on the fishing trip in May, and now there are never less than fifteen or sixteen people. There seem to be more every year. She loves the house bursting at the seams.

I don't have to worry about the cooking. The chef from Clarence House comes for one half of the trip, and then the chef from Royal Lodge comes for the other half. Some of them do the Castle of Mey as well, and then come down here for about ten days. Then they change over and go back to London, and the others come up and finish off the trip. There is a very pleasant atmosphere in the house. It's just like one big happy family – everybody says that when they come in it. It just seems a very much lived-in house, which it is. On a nice day they all sit outside for tea, and Queen Elizabeth roams around in the garden, very much relaxed.

She's up pretty early in the morning, but she doesn't come down early – maybe at half past ten, eleven o'clock when she has her coffee. At half past twelve every day, except Sunday, she goes out picnicking. When there are guests, all the ladies go, because the men will be down fishing already. Or if the men are shooting, she'll meet up with them at lunch time. Sunday is the only day they are in for lunch. During the day if you meet her in the house she always stops and speaks about the weather, or whatever is going on or whoever is staying at that moment. She will say a few words about the people who have stayed, or mention if they are enjoying their holiday or the fishing, and how many fish they have had. You never avoid her if you see her coming – she doesn't like people to turn back and go in and shut a door, so as not to trouble her. They have a little fun in the evenings; they dance in the drawing room after dinner and enjoy it. Sometimes they go to the log cabin by the river and have dinner down there by candlelight. The steward goes and sets things up for them, and stands by in case she needs anything, but all the guests muck in and help.

She really does love this place and stays to the very last minute. When the weather is nice and she has got all her friends here, she just loves it. She is a fun-loving person, she likes a joke, and she likes to know all about what is going on locally. She is just a marvellous character. I don't suppose anybody will fill her shoes. She is really an awfully nice person to work for.

Racing

The Queen Mother was an immensely successful owner of steeplechasers for over forty years, and her knowledge of form equalled that of the professionals.

The Queen Mother at the Derby. Appearances at the great race meetings were a most pleasurable duty, though she agreed with those who said racing was ninety per cent disappointment.

Michael Oswald

Manager at the Royal Stud at Sandringham, and racing manager for the Queen Mother.

Queen Elizabeth has always been very interested in racing and always known a lot about it. Her own family, going back to the nineteenth century, had a great tradition in racing with the Earls of Strathmore and John Bowes. The King was also very keen on racing, and had a very good stud, and Queen Elizabeth was always very involved with that. I think it was the late Lord Mildmay, who was a famous amateur rider, who persuaded her to have a horse. He was a great friend of the late Peter Cazalet, one of the greatest jumping trainers of his day, who went on to train all her horses until he died. Queen Elizabeth started in partnership with the Queen – who was then Princess Elizabeth – with the steeplechaser Monaveen, who turned out to be a pretty good horse, and it went on from there. When the King died the present Queen carried on with his stud and stable, and the Queen Mother went into steeplechasing and hurdling, although steeplechasing is by far her favourite. I think she was probably attracted by the colourful and amusing people one meets in steeplechasing, and while the Queen was racing and breeding for the flat, she probably thought she'd do something different on her own.

She knows an awful lot about it now, and has been doing it with great success for over forty years. I think at the moment she's won about four hundred races – probably more than anybody else alive today. She knows all about the form of her own horses, and of the leading horses belonging to other people. Of course you don't win all the time – I think she agrees it's ninety per cent disappointment, but the other ten per cent is such fun it makes up for it. She loves the winning side of it, but she also likes the

The Queen Mother with Michael Oswald
(centre right) at Ascot in 1983.

people who work in the stables – the jockeys and the stable lads. She's the most unselfish owner you could imagine. She even prefers it if her horse isn't favourite, because if it is everybody then expects it's going to do well, and she worries if they're disappointed.

The greatest disappointment must have been when Devon Loch fell in the run up to the post in the Grand National. That was an unbelievable story, which nobody has properly explained, and I think it must have been a pretty sore point. I know she doesn't really like it to be talked about. It's been raked over time and time again, but she never mentions it. Certainly the National isn't one of her favourite races. When she does win a race she has the most tremendous reception, because she is so popular. I remember particularly the Whitbread Gold Cup with Special Cargo, who also won her three Grand Military Gold Cups. I'm sure there is a certain amount of betting on her horses for sentimental reasons. They probably start with a slightly shorter price because they're owned by her, and particularly if she's there.

We had one great afternoon at Sandown when Queen Elizabeth won three important races. She started off by winning the Grand Military Gold Cup – for the third time – with Special Cargo. So I sent a telegram to the Queen, who was at sea off the south coast of Australia in the Royal Yacht *Britannia*. Then she won the Imperial Cup, so I sent another telegram, even more excited and enthusiastic than the first. And then The Argonaut won her third cup. So I sent a third telegram. Now, imagining that the Queen would be asleep, I thought she would get all three telegrams at breakfast and open them in any order, which would take away some of the fun and excitement. But in fact the Queen was on deck watching, or trying to watch, Halley's Comet through the scudding clouds in a rather stormy sea. So the telegrams came through all in the right order, and lightened a rough and perhaps rather dreary night.

When the Queen Mother can't get to the races she reads the newspapers, and *The Sporting Life*, of course. She has television, but quite a lot of races are not televised, so she has this old-fashioned blower system at Clarence House, where you get a rather tired commentary telling you without any enthusiasm where the horses are in a race. But at least it enables her to follow it and see who's won. She's been a great enhancer of racing, as she is of so many other things in life. For her, racing should be fun, and she makes it fun for so many other people.

(*Above*) Wrapped up against the weather, on holiday in Norfolk.

(*Right*) With the Prince and Princess of Wales, and the impressario Lord Delfont, at the Royal Variety Performance in 1984.

(*Previous page*) Lord Snowdon's 1987 portrait of the Queen Mother.

(*Above*) The Queen Mother and the Princess of Wales on their way to the Trooping the Colour ceremony in 1985, before the Princess's troubled marriage became public knowledge.

(*Right*) A glittering event in 1983.

(Above) At the Royal Anglian Regiment in Colchester, one of the many windswept parade grounds visited by the Queen Mother. This picture was taken just before her 90th birthday.

(*Opposite*) The official portrait to mark the Queen Mother's 90th birthday, taken at Clarence House.

Another 90th birthday portrait, with her corgi, Ranger, in the garden at Clarence House.

With a favourite regiment, the Irish Guards, at Chelsea Barracks on St Patrick's day 1994.

A frivolous hat for the 96-year-old Queen Mother, photographed by her former son-in-law, Lord Snowdon.

(*Overleaf*) The Queen Mother at 97.

Dick Francis

The Queen Mother's jockey during the 1950s. He later became her favourite thriller writer, with a series of books about skullduggery in the racing world.

I rode dozens of times for the Queen Mother. One would often see her at the training stables when she came to stay with her trainer, Peter Cazalet. She would come out and watch the horses schooling before breakfast. At the race meeting she would occasionally go to see the horse being saddled up, but mostly she would walk into the parade ring, and one would go out there and join her and the trainer, and discuss the final tactics for the race. She was very knowledgeable. The first fancied horse I rode for the Queen Mother was at Lingfield way back in 1953. Wc thought we had an excellent chance, which we did, and Peter Cazalet said to me in the parade ring beforehand: 'Always lie third or fourth until you come to the last, kick him on, jump it in front and make the best of your way home.' I jumped the last fence in front, and half way up the straight I thought I was winning quite easily, because the horse was going so well. But suddenly I heard a terrific lot of noise and shouting from the sidelines, which is a thing jockeys don't hear normally, and I thought: 'My God, I'm being tackled.' I didn't dare look round, I just sat down and rode hard for the winning post. When I'd passed it I stood up in my irons and looked round, and the opposition was lengths and lengths back. It was in the early days of royal winners and the noise was just the crowd giving us a great reception.

That happened a number of times throughout my years riding for her, and one got used to it. Until this day in the Grand National. It's a four-and-a-half-mile race and I'd had a wonderful ride for four miles. There were quarter of a million people at Aintree that day, and as I jumped the last fence, I think 249,999 of them were cheering for the Queen Mother. You could hear this crescendo of cheering building up as I rode hard for the winning post. As we approached the outside of the water-jump, which we'd jumped OK the first time round, looking at the film – which I've done many times since – you see Devon Loch prick his ears. It was a sign of recognition: 'I was here last time round.' As he did that, the crescendo of cheering hit him: 'My God, what's that?' He'd never heard anything like it, and his hindquarters just refused to act. Down he goes on his belly, slides along the ground, all hope of winning the Grand National gone. I stayed on his back, and he got to his feet, and if I could have got him going then I was still far enough in front to have won. But he'd pulled all the muscles in his hindquarters, and I had to get off him and walk away in disgust. It was a terrible tragedy, but looking at it now I think it was Her Majesty's popularity that lost her that Grand National, because everyone was cheering for her. She was naturally very upset, although one couldn't detect it. She never lost that smile on her face. But I was dumbstruck. I had got off Devon Loch where it happened and started to walk back towards the changing room, and I could see everyone coming towards me to find out what had happened. Fortunately an ambulance drove past, and the fellow lowered his window and said: 'Jump in the back, mate.' I was never more glad to get in an ambulance in all my life. And he took me right round the back of the changing room and I went in that way. I sat there in a daze, and Peter Cazalet came in as much in a daze as I was. We sat and discussed it for a moment, and he said: 'Well I think you'd better just put on your jacket, and we'll go up and see the Royal Family.' They were all as flabbergasted as everyone else but Her Majesty was most philosophical. She said: 'Well, that's racing.' And my word, that was racing, or not racing. But she has had plenty of other winners, and she loved to celebrate. Even when the foot-and-mouth disease epidemic was on, and there was no racing, she had a party at Clarence House to cheer everyone up. She always has the first copy off the presses of my books, and it is wonderful to see them all in a line in the sitting room of Clarence House.

On the big occasions she always has parties. She had a dance at one of the big London hotels to celebrate her hundredth

Dick Francis with the Queen Mother
at the races in 1969. As a jockey
he often wore her racing silks.

winner. Everyone in the racing world and the theatre was there. After dinner Sir Martin Gilliat came up and said to me: 'Dick, the Queen Mother would like to have a few words with you.' And he grabbed Bill Rees, her current jockey at that time, and we both went over and sat with her for about twenty minutes. Suddenly who should come up but Kenneth More, the film star: 'Hello, Ma'am,' he said. 'How about a dance?' And she said: 'Oh, you go and sit down for a bit, I'm talking to my jockeys.' As we walked away afterwards Bill Rees said to me: 'He was a bit cheeky coming up and butting in, asking for a dance.' I said: 'Well, we'd better ask her ourselves.' He said: 'Well, you go and ask her.' So I went and asked Her Majesty to have a dance, and after we'd danced, I think she danced with all the other jockeys as well. She loves dancing. She has got up at other parties, when there's a carpet on the floor, and danced to the Scottish tunes which she loves. At one of the parties the Queen and Princess Margaret went home soon after midnight, but the Queen Mother was there until the early hours of the morning, entirely enjoying it.

She loves life and she loves steeplechasing. It's more of a sport than a business, unlike flat racing, although the two do mix a little bit more these days. The Queen Mother loves the sporting aspect of steeplechasing and the sport owes her a massive debt for all the enthusiasm she has put into it.

Mrs Fulke Walwyn

Her husband trained the Queen Mother's horses after the death of Peter Cazalet. The Queen Mother often came down to the Walwyns' training establishment at Lambourn.

We already knew the Queen Mother, because she used to go racing a lot, and she used to present a lot of cups, which we luckily sometimes won. We also knew Peter Cazalet very well. He trained her horses when she started. We didn't have any idea that we would train for her when Peter died. I think there was an idea that she might give up having horses in training. I don't know what changed her mind, but she decided to go on and, marvellously, she chose us to train for her.

She usually has eight to ten horses in training during a season. It varies a bit, and one or two may go back in the middle of the season. They're all steeplechasers, because I think she finds steeplechasing more sporting than flat racing, and she finds the people nice. The horses stay in training much longer as well, because they run to a much greater age. She becomes friends with them, and she likes having them back at Sandringham when they've retired. They also go back there for their summer holidays when they've finished the season, for about three months. She likes having them around which you can't really do with flat-race horses.

Some people like flat racing because it's in the summer, whereas steeplechasing is in the winter, but she doesn't seem to mind what the weather is. She'll always go down to the paddock to see the horse, and if it's in the first three she'll go back after the race to pat him and say, 'Well done'. However hard it's raining she'll come out and hardly bother with a mackintosh. She's absolutely extraordinary.

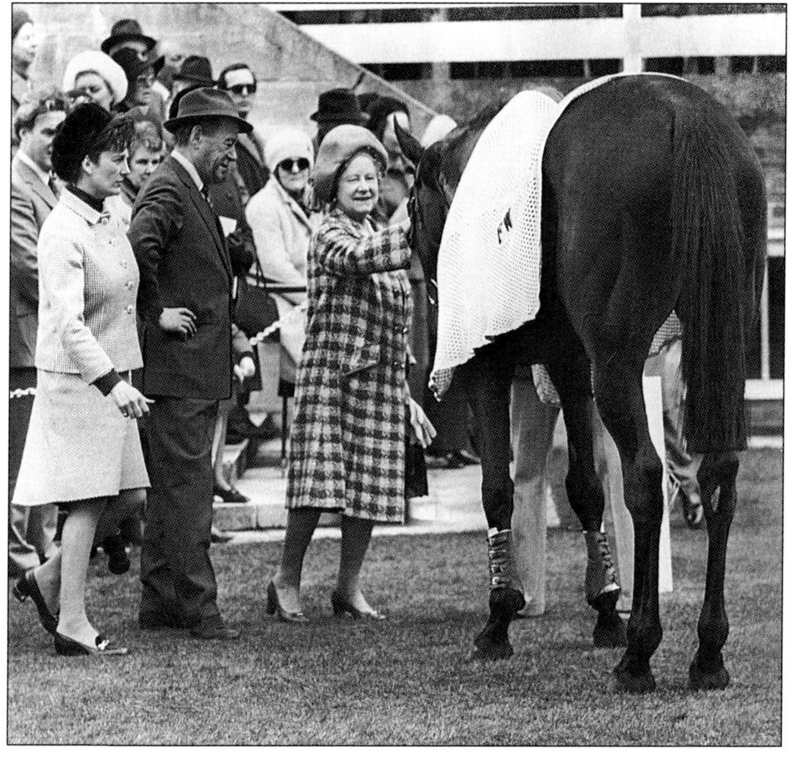

Mr and Mrs Fulke Walwyn with
the Queen Mother and Isle of Man,
one of her many steeplechasers.

She so obviously enjoys it, and gets very excited watching, especially if it's a close race like the famous Whitbread that she won with Special Cargo. It was a terribly close finish. Three horses, and nobody knew which had won. She was so excited she wouldn't move until she knew. Luckily it was her horse, by a short head. It was an amazing race, one of the highlights of her racing life. Special Cargo is a favourite of hers. It ran in the Grand Military Gold Cup three years running, which is an amazing thing to do. One year we had an unfortunate mishap, because we ran two horses; Sun Rising, for the Queen Mother, and this other horse who'd only just come to us. The one race that his owner wanted to run this horse in was the Grand Military, so we ran it.

It was 33–1 and we didn't think it had a chance, and blimey if it didn't go and beat Sun Rising, who was second. Afterwards we didn't know where to go in the unsaddling enclosure. Eventually Fulke went to the second-placed horse – the Queen Mother's – and I went to the winner. She was actually very funny about it. We said to her: 'It's extraordinary, we just can't believe it. We very nearly didn't run the winner because he wasn't right two days ago.' So she said: 'I wish you hadn't run him.' But she was fine afterwards. She always has a party after the Grand Military and she'd got over it by then, although I don't think we had!

Philip Delaney

Grocer in Cheltenham, whose shop became an unlikely port of call for the Queen Mother on her visits to the Cheltenham Race Meeting.

Back in 1969 I had a shop in another part of Cheltenham. I knew the royal car would pass it on the way to the race course, and being a great royalist, I decided to stand outside the shop and wave a Union Jack. A few of my customers knew I was patriotic, and they asked if I could tell them the approximate time. I told them that it would be about half past four, but Her Majesty left a little bit earlier, and sailed past the shop ten or fifteen minutes before. Of course they were all very annoyed with me, and I wasn't the most popular person in Cheltenham.

The following year they asked whether I could get it right, so I was cheeky and I wrote to her Private Secretary, Sir Martin Gilliat, and explained what had happened. He wrote back and said that Her Majesty was very sorry to have missed a lot of people, but that she would be sure to slow down the following year. He gave me an exact timing a little nearer the actual date. So I arranged for the children of the local school, a lot of old people and customers to be outside ready for the royal car to go past. I gave some flags to the children to hold, but I didn't have enough, so I grabbed some wild daffodils I was selling from a bucket, gave one to each child, and told them to throw it at the car as Her Majesty went past. I still had a great armful of these wild daffodils as the car approached. The police escort sailed past the shop, and true to her word the Queen Mother slowed down. To my surprise the car stopped and the door opened. I went forward and knelt in the back of Her Majesty's car, and she greeted me by name and said: 'Mr Delaney, are those flowers for me?' I passed them forward and said: 'Oh, yes certainly, Ma'am.

I'm sorry they're not orchids and carnations and the flowers that you're used to.' They weren't even done up in a bouquet; they were just loose. As I handed them to Her Majesty, some of them fell and the slime from the stems went over Her Majesty's skirt and over the Duchess of Beaufort's, who was sitting alongside her. I got my handkerchief out and was mopping down her skirt, and Her Majesty roared with laughter.

Meanwhile the police, having gone a long way up the road, suddenly realised they didn't have the royal car behind them and zoomed back. The children were sticking their noses against the windows, but when the police came down to try to pull them off the car, she stopped them and said: 'No, let them enjoy it.' We had a few minutes talk. I was full of apologies, but the Queen Mother said: 'Don't worry, the flowers are just what I like.'

To my surprise, the following year I had a letter to say that Her Majesty would call at such-and-such a time. I got a slightly more formal bouquet of flowers, and I also learnt from one of my customers that Her Majesty was very fond of peppermints. So I grabbed a packet of Polos from the shelf at the shop and gave it to her with the bouquet. She was thrilled about this, and said: 'I don't know how you knew that I liked peppermints.' And every year since then I have given her not only a few flowers, but a box of her favourite mints.

She has got such a charming smile, and no matter where she is or what the occasion, she will always give you a wonderful smile. She's so warm and generous in the way that she approaches everybody. She knows all about you before you meet her. You worry about what you're going to say, but as soon as she steps out of the car and shakes your hand, she leads you with the questions so you don't have to worry at all.

When I had to move I thought I wouldn't see her again, so in the March before I left I explained that it would be the last occasion I would meet her. She was very upset and said: 'Now, whereabouts are you going?' I said: 'Well, I'm staying in Cheltenham to manage the bakery stores in Prestbury.' And Her Majesty said: 'Well, if you're staying in Cheltenham I'm still coming to see you, because this is a tradition that's got to continue. When I come to the Gold Cup Meeting I'm going to be sure and see you.' I said: 'But it's rather a long way out.' But she said: 'It doesn't matter how far it is, I'll still come.' She now makes a detour of five or six miles to come to see us and it is wonderful that she still does.

Every year is special to me and has got its memories. About six or seven years ago my father had a heart attack and she was very concerned. The following year, much to my surprise, the first thing that Her Majesty said to me was: 'How is your father? I do hope he's better.' I was overwhelmed that she had remembered.

I had a customer who attended an exhibition in the Midlands which the Queen Mother was opening. She was wandering around the stalls and went over to my customer, who was running one, and asked her where she came from. When she said Cheltenham, the Queen Mother said, quite spontaneously: 'I've got a friend in Cheltenham, a Mr Delaney. Do you know him by any chance?' She had remembered my name out of the hundreds that she must meet, and that is a treasured memory as well.

Philip Delaney making his annual gift of flowers and mints to the Queen Mother.

Entertainment

The Queen Mother was a lifelong theatre-goer, with a particular fondness for performers who could make her laugh.

The Queen Mother at the Royal Opera House, Covent Garden, in 1966 for a Gala Performance in aid of the Royal Opera House Benevolent Fund.

EIIR

Lord Delfont

Show business impresario, whose long association with the Royal Variety Performance brought him into close contact with the Queen Mother.

I first met the Queen Mother in 1958. I have had the pleasure of meeting her for the past thirty years or more in connection with the Royal Variety Performance, as well as on many other occasions, mostly charity functions.

She is remarkably knowledgeable about show business. I remember a sherry party at Windsor Castle on a Sunday afternoon. The Queen Mother and I had a little chat, and during the conversation she said: 'Isn't it a shame about Frankie?' I was a bit nonplussed, so I queried it. 'Well,' she said, 'haven't you heard? Frankie Howerd's show is a failure in America. But he got very good reviews.' I was quite astonished that she had the news before I did.

She particularly likes comedians and speciality acts, jugglers, dancers, anything like that. But by and large she seems to enjoy every kind of entertainment, and is a great patron of the theatrical profession. I've asked her on many occasions if she would support a certain charity for me, and she has agreed. The last one she appeared at for me was in the West End for the Bud Flanagan Leukaemia Appeal. Of course she loved the Crazy Gang, and whenever we meet on the steps of the Palladium she always says: 'Oh, it's lovely to come back – the Palladium always brings back memories of the Crazy Gang, and particularly Flanagan and Allen.' I think she had a special affection for them, and they were able to do what no other comedians could at that time. They would almost address the Royal Box, and she liked it. She was very fond of them. On one occasion they threw a bunch of keys up to the box, because they said someone had left a car outside with the number HRH 1. They were never rude to the Royal Family, of course, just a bit boisterous. I think they like a bit of honest vulgarity, as George Robey, an old comedian, used to call it. I'm sure she enjoys a bit of that.

She is very kind and considerate too. I remember quite a number of years ago, when Tommy Steele was the first rock-and-roll artist we put into a Royal Variety Performance. Everybody was very worried about it, and after the first number Tommy said: 'Now, come on everybody, put your hands together.' But unfortunately nobody did, and there was quite a hush over the audience. So the Queen Mother leant out of her box, put her hands together, and it was fine after that. A marvellous gesture by her, but she is marvellous at that sort of thing.

I remember 1986 was the first year that the Duchess of York came along with the Queen Mother, which was rather nice. I had never met her before. I had arranged the seats in the boxes in the normal position – the Queen Mother sits in the centre and the other members of the Royal Family, if they are there, sit on either side of her. When we walked into the box and I pointed to the seat for Her Majesty to occupy, she said: 'No,' and she pointed to the Duchess of York. And so the Duchess sat down there, and the house really gave a tremendous burst of applause. It was a lovely gesture.

I did once introduce my mother to her, after many years of resisting it. My mother used to ring me every year and say: 'Am I being introduced this year?' And I would say: 'No, it's not possible, because it would look a bit strange.' But when she got to about eighty-six or eighty-seven, she rang me and said: 'All the neighbours are beginning to talk. They think there must be something wrong with me.' So I gave in, and rang the Queen Mother's Secretary and said: 'Is it all right to introduce my mother?' And he said: 'Of course it's all right.' When the time came I was walking up the stairs with Her Majesty, and she said: 'I understand I'm to meet your mother.' And I said: 'Yes, and very proud she is to meet you.' I had already warned my mother just to give her the bouquet of flowers and not say anything, but the Queen Mother came up to her and said: 'I'm very pleased to meet you, Mrs Grade. You must be very proud of your children.'

Lord Delfont with the Queen Mother in 1961.
His long association with the Royal Variety Performance
brought them into regular contact.

And my mother clasped both her hands and said: 'And you must be very proud of yours.' The Queen Mother didn't laugh at the time, of course, but when we got to the top of the stairs she said: 'I thought it was very amusing, and your mother is a lovely character.'

Later I had a video show at the Trocadero, in London, about the history of London. Part of it showed the Queen Mother in the East End during the blitz. Apparently at that time she said: 'The King is going to stay in London, and I will stay too.' I thought she might be interested in this show, so I arranged for her to come along, quite unofficially, and with no publicity. She arrived without any fuss, and I sat with her in the Trocadero. When this particular bit came on she was very moved, and a few minutes later she was wiping tears from her eyes.

Frankie Howerd

Comedian whose idiosyncratic humour appealed to the Queen Mother. He was her guest on several occasions.

I have been in show business many, many years – too many I think sometimes – but we have an expression, 'a good pro'. That really means somebody who is very conscientious, who goes on stage if he is not feeling so good, who works hard, who aims high and is dependable and does his stuff. I think that the Queen Mother is the supreme professional. She is admired as such by every pro that I know. She is undoubtedly a superstar, and when it comes to fulfilling her public duties, she is quite brilliant. She manages to combine sensitivity, a sense of humour, and a great sense of doing the right thing.

She has a way of noticing people at the right time, and saying the right thing to them. It's not easy because you have to ad lib, which I find very difficult. If you rehearse, you can learn everything off by heart, but when you are meeting people all the time, your mind has to work like a sort of radar system. To pick up the vibrations so as always to say the right thing requires great sensitivity, and an acute perception, which she has got to a tremendous degree.

To my knowledge, she is a master of not saying the wrong thing. I have been, if you can use the word, a public figure, and one can easily say the wrong thing. I have made some terrible gaffes. I remember when I was first asked to meet the Queen Mother – she was the Queen then – and I went to Buckingham Palace to perform at a staff party. I was petrified, because I had only been in show business a couple of years. From being a poor boy in the army, I was suddenly meeting the Royal Family and that was very overwhelming for me.

Frankie Howerd meets one of his greatest fans
at the Royal Variety Performance in 1966.

There were three artists, and I didn't think I was very good. I was so edgy. Afterwards I got ready to say: 'Your Majesty', and all that sort of thing, as much protocol as I could manage, being a bit uncouth. And the Queen Mother darted over to me and said: 'Oh, I am so pleased, and so thrilled to meet you.' Anyway I chatted away to her and I told her a long story. I began to think I would never get to the end of this wretched story, but she was so patient, and looked interested all the time. Just as I got near the end, up came King George VI, and she said: 'Oh, darling, Mr Howerd is telling me such an interesting story.' So I had to start right from the beginning and go through it again. She was a model of patience. I would have gone mad if it had been me.

I also noticed something else. She was dressed very simply. She didn't dress above the staff who were there – no great tiaras, no great diamonds – and I thought that was very tactful. She was so homely, and I thought if only I could have met her and the King before I did the show, I would have been a hundred times better.

That was the first time, and since then, of course, I have met her a number of times. She is very interested in show business and understands the nerves, and the things that go on. She said to me one night after the Royal Variety Show: 'So relaxed tonight, wasn't it? Very relaxed atmosphere.' She was right, because not all the shows were relaxed; some people are a bag of nerves, but this was a particularly relaxed night and she sensed it straight away.

She is a good audience because she understands the effort that has been put into a show, and she goes to enjoy it and to meet it more than half way. She doesn't go just to sit there and say: 'Well now, make me laugh.' She goes there wanting to laugh, to be encouraging, which is a performer's dream, because show business is tough going. One of the things you have to accept is rejection. I did a show over in America and we were extremely unlucky and it flopped. Naturally I was very upset. There were items in the press over here about it, and the Queen Mother spoke to Lord Delfont and said that she'd read about it and how sorry she was. She said she hoped I wasn't taking it too badly, and wasn't too upset. I was very touched by that. She understands artists.

This sounds awfully conceited, but I went to a lunch with her at somebody's house and she told me I was her favourite comedian. And typical of me, saying the wrong thing, instead of just saying 'Thank you,' and being good-mannered like anybody else would've been, I was so surprised, I said: 'Well, I'm glad somebody is.' I thought: 'What have I said?' But it made her grin.

Afterwards we were sitting on a settee in the lounge and talking about moral courage, in which she was very interested. Dame Rebecca West, who was a famous writer, and was then ninety-one, was also at the luncheon party. Her legs weren't good and she was very, very deaf, and she was sitting alone in an armchair because it was the most comfortable place. While Queen Elizabeth was talking to me she suddenly saw Rebecca West sitting there all alone, looking rather forlorn, so she said: 'Will you excuse me a moment?' So I stood up, and she belted across and knelt on the floor beside Rebecca West, and got involved in this animated conversation. She was very sensitive to the fact that Rebecca West was on her own.

My manager took me down there for that luncheon, and he met the Queen Mother before lunch, and then went away. When he came back afterwards he brought her a big box of chocolates. I glared at him because I thought it wasn't protocol, but she took the box and said: 'Well, that's very kind of you.' I said to him later: 'You shouldn't have done that. You're not supposed to. You should have at least curtsied or bowed or followed some sort of protocol.' But she took it all in her stride. She had a long chiffon handkerchief in her favourite powder blue, and when she was leaving she held it out of the car like a flag in the breeze, waving goodbye. We were all laughing until we realised that in the rush she had forgotten this box of chocolates, and a little gift the staff had given her. Naturally we thought we would send them on to her, but lo and behold, back came the car. She'd got to Windsor Castle, which wasn't all that far away, and then sent the car back for them. I thought it was a very nice thing to do.

It has been a wonderful privilege to have her as a fan. I couldn't be more thrilled. I was, I tell you in all modesty, very surprised when I found out. I've always admired the Queen Mother. She's been a part of my life, someone I looked up to. She has great charisma; something shines, like a sort of radiance – it's very remarkable. I mentioned that when I was at this lunch we talked seriously, and I think underneath she's a very strong-minded woman. I am talking about principles, and duty and courage. And at the end of it all, with her homeliness and sensitivity, and the laughter and ability to make one feel relaxed, one is always still aware that she is the Queen Mother.

Sir Peter Ustinov

Actor, writer, mimic and raconteur, he met the Queen Mother many times, both socially and through their connection with Dundee University.

Our first meeting was when she asked me to lunch. I remember she rather playfully offered me toffee. Now I don't know many people who do that after lunch, and the toffee looked very voluptuous and is the sort of thing I'm not allowed. But I had to take it; I felt obliged. Then as soon as the toffee was in my mouth, she asked me a question about the collected works of James Joyce, or T. S. Eliot or someone, and that was when both rows of teeth were engaged irrevocably with this piece of toffee. She enjoyed that enormously. She knew what she was doing, I'm sure. It wasn't fudge, it was toffee.

Her lunches at Clarence House are very spectacular. They are neither formal nor informal, because they are in the shadow of Buckingham Palace and yet you feel that you are in some lodge in the grounds. They are very delicious, but she is a very delicious woman. She would be able to convert even the most rabid republican into at least a mild royalist, because she behaves as somebody who knows her responsibilities, and at the same time has moments when she will break out of that in order to relax. If you are asked to share those moments, it's very flattering.

She is a tremendous giggler and a great blusher. I met her again at the opening of Dundee University, where I was elected the first Rector and she was the Chancellor. It was in 1968, at the worst time of student difficulties. France was in complete revolt, there was an air of revolution and irreverence everywhere and a lot of iconoclastic behaviour. As we arrived in a solemn procession the students pelted us with toilet rolls. They kept hold of one end, like streamers at a ball, and threw the other end. The

Queen Mother stopped and picked these up as though somebody had misplaced them. 'Was this yours? Oh, could you take it?' And it was her sang-froid and her absolute refusal to be shocked by this, which immediately silenced all the students. She knows instinctively what to do on those occasions. She doesn't rise to being heckled at all; she just pretends it must be an oversight on the part of the people doing it.

The way she reacted not only showed her presence of mind, but was so charming and so disarming, even to the most rabid element, that she brought peace to troubled waters. I think some of the men would have been taking names, which wouldn't have been the way to do it. She is a wonderful mollifier, but at the same time she doesn't give away anything of her integrity in doing so.

She took her responsibilities as Chancellor very seriously, but she loved the safety valve of a giggle on the side, or a stray remark which would ease tensions and put situations to rights. In fact so seriously did she take her responsibilities, that she sat through the whole of my speech as Rector, which I thought was miraculous, because even I found difficulty in doing that. She said it was quite good, and I must say it was one of my better efforts. I have never borrowed from it for future occasions. I thought it was sacrosanct. Another time we had to open the new dental school, of which Dundee was extremely proud. It was very modern, with the most up-to-date equipment in the British Isles. I looked at the plans just before she cut the tape, and I went up to her and said very softly: 'I think, Ma'am, the architect was inspired by Burke and Hare, the body snatchers of Edinburgh.' She said: 'What do you mean?', and I pointed out that there were three departments on the penthouse level – one was Emergency, next door was Post-mortem, and next door to that was Experimental. She said: 'I see what you mean,' and cut the tape rather quickly.

On her eightieth birthday, I told one or two of these tales from the stage. I couldn't see the reaction because she was plunged in the darkness of her box, but she was very cordial afterwards. She looked at me slightly as though I had perhaps remembered the wrong things about her, but her look was not very seriously meant. It was mildly admonishing: 'Oh, you are wicked.'

Sir Peter Ustinov as Rector of Dundee University
and the Queen Mother as Chancellor.

I was asked to Chequers for something in honour of the Queen Mother. She wanted me to be there, which was very nice of her, and I came almost directly from Osaka in Japan, where I had been on a mission for the High Commissioner for Refugees. I brought with me some Japanese smoked salmon, which I gave to Mrs Thatcher. I said: 'This is not a gift in the normal sense. There is no effort to corrupt you, Prime Minister; I just wanted as a patriotic duty to show you that Japanese are attacking all along the line, not merely with motor cars and transistors, but also with smoked salmon.' And the Queen Mother said: 'You are not going to pretend that it's better than our Scottish smoked salmon, are you?' And I said, in a stage Japanese accent: 'With your permission, we sink so!' She laughed and said: 'Oh, you are a fool.'

She is redolent of all the niceties of another age, and yet

disregards them completely. Her real person is always in tune with the times, that's what I feel. Sometimes her behaviour seems to be so well brought up as to be no longer quite valid, but then she says something which makes it clear that she knows what she is doing. It is useless to try and pretend you are the same age as young people in order to ingratiate yourself with them; it's not what they want. They want somebody of a different generation. I have always thought that parents are people on whom the young puppies cut their teeth; sometimes it is a very painful process, but it is absolutely necessary, and I think she knows that too. She behaves in a kind of Kate Greenaway nursery tea way, but there is something very different underneath, which is watching, observing, and coming to its conclusions. She is always unflappable, and always with a tendency to be amused rather than embarrassed. I have never seen her embarrassed. I don't know what she would do. She is capable of riding any sort of wave that comes along and coming out the other side looking exactly as she did when she went in. I admire her enormously, and I think she is probably – I don't mean any disrespect to the others – the most consistently popular member of the Royal Family. She does a great deal for that family as a kind of anchor.

She has a great love of popular entertainment, and that is a safety valve on the whole edifice of State. She humanises everything she touches, and if there is a low comedian around, she will probably laugh more heartily at what goes on than most people. Many of them are rather nervous about that, and will look at her to see how she reacts before letting their own sense of fun go. In that way she is a very good influence in getting everybody relaxed. An extraordinary pool of calmness seems to spread around her. She has been through a lot in her life, as the Queen, and as the widow of a King – all the things that everybody probably goes through, but in her case in a very public way. But she has never wavered, and always comes out smiling. As such, she is a wonderful example of true constancy.

Although the Castle of Mey was the Queen Mother's home for only a few weeks each year, she was accepted by the Caithness people as 'one of us'.

The Castle of Mey

The Queen Mother bought the castle after her husband George VI died in 1952. On the far north coast of mainland Britain, looking across the Pentland Firth towards the Orkneys, Mey was the only house she ever actually owned. It was her favourite among all her residences.

Viscount Thurso

Owner of Thurso Castle in Caithness. Thurso is the nearest town to the Castle of Mey.

I first met her when she had made up her mind to buy the Castle of Mey. My wife and I were invited to dinner by a neighbour, Lady Doris Vyner, and we were told that we were going to hear a very interesting announcement. Queen Elizabeth was at the dinner party, and she told us that she had met this beautiful old castle and fallen in love with it, that it needed a friend and she was going to be its friend and restore it to health. I think what appealed to her was partly its character, but also the fact that it needed somebody. At that stage the King had just died, and I think she needed somebody too. Here was a little castle with character, and she felt that if she loved it, it would love her back. And indeed it has – the whole county has.

She has been accepted – it sounds presumptuous to say – by the people of Caithness as a Caithness person, which is an enormous compliment. It means that she has been taken to all of their hearts in a very special way. She has also put Caithness on the map; people know where Mey is and where Caithness is. If you say you live somewhere near John O'Groats, people have a vague idea where that is, but if you say you live in Caithness where the Queen Mother lives, where the Castle of Mey is, people understand instantly.

Coming from Angus, she is a bit of a southerner to us, but she is very Scottish and she understands Scottish people, and there is an immediate rapport that needs no words said. Caithness people are very proud that she chose to live here. They took it as an enormous compliment, and so it was. They felt that here at last was the true recognition of the worth which they always knew existed – the final seal of approval of Caithness.

In Scotland we approach things differently from the way English people do. Queen Elizabeth was always aware of the differences in relationships, politics, religion, and all these things that are so much part of who one is and where one lives. It was always easy for her to understand how people's minds work up here, and how they live. Everyone was aware at once that she knew what we were talking about.

When she comes to Mey it's like a mini season. It used to be a fairly private visit, but now it has grown and all sorts of things happen. People who are away make a point of coming home at this time of year, the cocktail parties take place, and houses are dusted out and warmed up for the occasion. But she is the leading light. She has wonderful picnics beside the river, and on one occasion when we went fishing with her we had the most magnificent alfresco meal I have ever had in my life. We had tables and chairs and we sat down to everything from a Martini to start with, down to a little liqueur to end up with. We had warm food, which is amazing for a picnic, and we took plenty of time over it. Usually one sits on the river bank with a cold sandwich and that's it, but not at all with Queen Elizabeth. It was a real meal.

She is a keen fisherwoman, and a very good one. She throws a lovely line and has that essential quality for a good and successful fisherwoman; that is to throw the extra little cast, give it another little flick – in other words to keep trying, keep the fly in the water. She will fish on even when it doesn't look very promising,

Viscount Thurso and the Queen Mother await the arrival of the Queen at Scrabster harbour.

and she gets her reward as a result. What attracts her to fishing is partly the peace of it. You are away from everything else, and you are by a river, which is a living thing. You are also with people, with great characters. Fishermen are all characters, whether they are toffs or ghillies, and she enjoys that. She finds them amusing, with their interest in the sport, and in the life of the fish and nature.

She can talk to anybody, from the ghillie to the terribly grand, from the small child to the old man of a hundred. All of us feel at home with her. She has such a good sense of humour that she can overlook our failings because they are amusing. She will forgive us an awful lot, provided we are contributing to society, or to the party, or whatever it may happen to be. She can find something in everybody, though I suppose she sees through the charlatans. She probably feels a bit cold towards some people, even if she doesn't show it, but if there is anything to warm towards, she will find it. I went round a hospital with her last year, and it was wonderful the way she spoke to everybody and they all seemed to be able to speak so easily to her. It's quite remarkable when you think that people in hospital are not actually in the most receptive mood. If you are lying there feeling as sick as a dog, you don't want to make small talk, so it's a gift to be able to draw people out in the way that she does. I'm sure all the patients felt a lot better.

Her other interest up here is in livestock, and not only in her own. She takes a real interest in the breeds. The Aberdeen Angus Cattle Society will be the first to acknowledge that she has been an enormous help to them. She has opened up her farm at Longo for farm walks, which have been very successful in publicising the breed, and showing what is being done at Mey. She is very fond of her cows, and I think probably second to meeting people up here, it's her farming enterprise that holds her interest.

My lasting memory of her will be as a whole person – her charm, her kindness, her enthusiasm, all these things, but all in one person. I can visualise her completely as I speak, and that is the way I shall always remember her.

Martin Leslie

Factor (land agent) for the Queen at Balmoral, and for the Queen Mother at the Castle of Mey.

I usually come up to the Castle of Mey once a month. The responsibilities are divided into two halves. There is the estate side, principally the fabric of the castle, which is of a considerable age and built of quite porous sandstone, so we have quite a lot of trouble in keeping the damp out. Then there is the farming side, with the pedigree Aberdeen Angus herd and the pedigree North Country Cheviot sheep flock. Her Majesty takes a very great interest in them. When she's in residence she walks every day, sometimes twice a day, and looks at the cattle and the sheep that are near the castle. And she will pay visits to her farm, Longo Farm, which is just along the coast here.

She enjoys hearing the details of the agricultual shows and sales, and how we have got on. She is very enthusiastic about the successes, and very understanding when things don't go quite so well. Her Majesty has done very well at the local shows and also at the Royal Highland show over the years. She has won quite a few prizes.

It is amazing that she takes such a close interest in it all. We must be on the periphery of her experience, but I have a standing order to telephone every time I come up here, either in the evening, or in the morning of the following day, and then discuss the affairs of the estate and farm in detail. She wants to know how the people are, how the stock are looking, what Caithness is looking like and if the weather is fine and the skies are beautiful, as they are very often.

Going around with Her Majesty I get the feeling that it's the space, the ever-changing skies, and the people that she particularly loves about this place. I think the Castle of Mey is also very special to her because it's the only place that she actually owns. She renovated the castle, and indeed probably saved it from coming down. She furnished it, resurrected the garden and made it into a show-piece, which has given enjoyment, not just to Her Majesty, but to many people who come here on garden opening days.

Her interests are so wide and yet she is concerned about the smallest thing as well. Her powers of observation are second to

Martin Leslie (far right) and Viscount Thurso join the Queen Mother and other guests for one of the Queen Mother's great passions – a reel.

none, about places, people and things. We have had visits up here from farming organisations like the Aberdeen Angus Cattle Society, of which Her Majesty is patron, and the Smithfield Club, of which she's a Vice-President, and the farmers are amazed to discover that she is so knowledgeable and interested in the farm. It's something wonderful to behold, as a grin splits the face of the farmer that she is talking to.

I once went to Canada with Her Majesty. She was opening the fifth World Angus Forum and had suggested that I should attend. That experience fortified all the feelings we have had over the years up here of her interest in places and people. Above all, I remember her stamina; she greets people at the end of a long day in exactly the same way as at the beginning of the day, with intense interest in what they are doing and what they feel. It's wonderful to be even on the very fringe of it, and observe it. There was an atmosphere which, unless you are fortunate enough to experience it, is very difficult to describe. The immense feeling everybody had for Her Majesty was almost a tangible thing.

It is her enjoyment of places and people and things that I will remember most, and everything overlayed with humour sometimes to the point of merriment. She will stop and talk to anybody that she meets around here about all sorts of things. It makes everybody's day when Her Majesty talks to them.

Mrs Hetty Munro

Till 1989 the owner of an antique shop in Thurso, Caithness, at which the Queen Mother was a regular customer.

The first time I met Queen Elizabeth was the year after she came to Caithness. She came into the old shop – we had a smaller one then – and we have been very lucky because she has come into the shop every year since. They do say that Her Majesty has the most wonderful memory, and it's true. One day she was in the shop and we had a little French leather case with four bottles in. Her Majesty commented on it, because it was really a very beautiful piece. About five years later she came into the shop and we had another one – not the duplicate, but similar – and she said: 'Oh, that's just like the one I saw here about five years ago.' No one could have prompted her for that, and just think of what she'd seen in five years. I certainly wouldn't have remembered something like that.

We never tell anyone what the Queen Mother buys, but she buys what she likes. They are presents and things like that, and she's got some of our things in the castle. We are very honoured to be asked to parties there, which is an enormous privilege and very enjoyable. Privileges aren't always enjoyable, but this one is. Her manner is totally natural, completely magic. You know that when Queen Elizabeth is talking to you, that is the only thing she is interested in in the world.

I don't know why she fell in love with Caithness, maybe because it was different. It's a totally different part of Scotland to Balmoral, or Edinburgh, or the Western Isles. It's a land of the big sky. She loves it here. She has her prize flock of sheep and her prize herd of Aberdeen Angus cows, and she is very proud of both of them. Another thing is that we don't bother her. A lot of people do, but we don't. I think she maybe notices that we are a little more polite than some others. We don't push and pry, and she feels much freer to be able to wonder round the county. I think that has quite a lot to do with it. When she goes on picnics to one of the better-known beaches, nobody would dream of following her to look. Normally when she comes to the Caithness artists' exhibition, she comes in the morning, when it's closed. One year she couldn't make it and so she came in the afternoon when it was open. There were three people in the exhibition, and they took one look and they turned right on their heels and went out. They weren't asked, but that is Caithness. It may not be a good habit, but it's a useful habit at times.

The people who know her in Caithness just look on her as one of us. That's rude, isn't it? But it's not meant to be. It would be presumptuous to say she is a friend. You could never take her for granted, because she has always got this magic. You couldn't put it on for ten minutes without it being spotted. We've all met people who put on an act, and we give them a couple of seconds and just say: 'Phoney.' But in her case it's real. When she walks into a room every eye turns. She doesn't do anything, she just walks in.

Ian and Margie Sinclair

Violinist and singer in the Scottish tradition, who put on ceilidhs (musical evenings) for the Queen Mother at the Castle of Mey.

MARGIE SINCLAIR:

The first time we played for her at Mey, we arrived when they were at dinner. We expected to be shepherded up the back stairs, to tune up before going through to perform as the cabaret. But instead it was in through the front door, with everybody helping to carry cases – her secretary and the equerries. We found ourselves in this room which turned out to be the Queen Mother's den. It was: 'Would this be all right? Is there plenty of room? Will you manage to tune up here?' We were quite amazed at this.

There are folding doors in this room, and Lady Fermoy, I think it was, came through and said: 'Would you like to start the proceedings off?' David Stevens, a piper friend of ours, went through to where they were sitting. The doors had been left ajar, so I had a wee look through just to see what the layout was for when I went through myself. The first person who caught my eye was the Queen Mother, sitting directly opposite me in an armchair. Her feet were tapping away and her eyes were just twinkling, and immediately I felt at ease. I thought: 'This is a party; it's not formal.'

So we gave our performance, and at the end she came forward and was introduced to each of us in turn. As she came along she stopped and spoke to each of us. We were all fairly formal – I sort of bobbed, and said: 'Ma'am.' Then she came to Ray, a member of the group who is a physicist, and like most scientists, slightly in another world. He said: 'I believe we have met before.' And she said: 'Really, when was that?' He said: 'You're Chancellor of the university I was at.' We were thinking what a daft thing to say to the Queen Mother – the thousands of folk she must have met. But she just asked right away 'What year was that?' And he got so caught up in this discussion with her that the formality just melted away.

When she came to the end of the line I expected her to just glide out of the door, but she smiled to us, opened the door and in rushed the corgis. She said: 'I didn't dare let them in before because they might have howled when the pipers were playing.' She had this twinkle in her eye and I could see she had her tongue in her cheek. At that point Ian bent down to pat the dog, but she said: 'I wouldn't do that if I were you. That's George – he's the one that gets the bad press.' It was just the way you would normally be if you have animals in the house; put them out of the way when visitors are there so that they're not a nuisance, but once everything is relaxed let them in. That set the atmosphere for the evening. It was totally relaxed and we all just mixed in.

IAN SINCLAIR:

She seemed to take to a song that I wrote, because she kept on singing it all night. It's called 'Tak' A Dram Afore Ye Go', and every time she came up to us she was singing, 'Tak' A Dram Afore Ye Go!' She is very knowledgeable about Scottish music. She said that it made her remember what it was like when she was young, and her father had been very keen on having evenings around the piano.

Once we played after she'd swallowed a fish bone and had been rushed to hospital in Aberdeen. We thought it would be off, but no, she came back and struggled through it, and that was another excellent night. It was all so natural again. The first time I went along, I was waiting to be spoken to, rather than speaking to her. But it was so informal that after maybe an hour, you'd just quite naturally turn round and start speaking to her. You forgot who she was and all the centuries of history around her. She was talking to me about my mother, who was born about two or

Ian and Margie Sinclair (back left).

three hundred yards from the castle. In a way she seemed like any old-age pensioner – she told me this year she'd just put in the central heating, and next year she would have to do something about the roof.

MARGIE SINCLAIR:

One thing that amazed me was when she said to one of our pipers: 'May I ask where you got those pipes? Would they happen to be Pipe Major somebody-or-other's presentation set?' He was totally astounded at this and said: 'Yes', and explained how they came into his possession. She said: 'I thought I recognised them.' She impressed me enormously. It was her presence, nothing to do with royalty. Anywhere you'd met that woman you would have been held by her, because she does have charisma. I know that is a sort of twee word nowadays, but she just has so much personality and she is quite ageless. I got the impression she is very at ease with young people; certainly most of the people there were young.

She just sparkles, and her eyes seem so young and full of mischief. You can see a twinkle when she has her tongue in her cheek. And when she is enjoying something, like a particular type of music, you've no doubt, because her eyes just light up, and sparkle and dance like violets.

IAN SINCLAIR:

The last time we were there, she said: 'We must have a photograph taken.' We duly sat down and got organised, and Brian put his camera on the tripod with the delay on it so that he could get into the picture as well. He went over to the Queen Mother and bent down and said: 'Now this is a very good camera and it has got a wee delay on it. You set the time and if you'd just look towards it there' – as if he was explaining it to his grandmother. Later we said to Brian: 'This is probably the most photographed woman in the world and you're telling her what to do with a camera.' But she just sat there and smiled at him and said: 'Yes, yes.'

MARGIE SINCLAIR:

Another thing about her is her femininity, the sort of femininity that comes through regardless of what you are wearing, or how your hair looks. She has this lovely grace about her, and I couldn't get over how light she was on her feet in those high heels. At the time of her eightieth birthday celebrations she had had a tremendous amount of public engagements, and when we went to the castle her staff were trying to keep it low key so that she didn't get too excited and burn the midnight oil. They thought that it might prove a terrific strain, but she wasn't having that at all. There she was very late at night on these high heels, with a lovely, soft feminine dress, gliding around the room. You could almost imagine that she would just blow in the wind, she's so featherlike.

IAN SINCLAIR:

I think she must have a tremendous memory, because the first time we were there one of the servants came with a trolley of drinks and she asked everybody what they wanted. It was all whisky or vodka, but one member of the group, a young lad, said: 'Have you got a can of McEwan's Export?' She said: 'Oh, I'll get one.' So someone went away and came back with this can.

The next time we went along, there were three cans of McEwan's Export on the trolley, so somebody must have remembered.

MARGIE SINCLAIR:

Once when they came down with sausage rolls, and bits and pieces for supper, Sir Martin Gilliat, her Private Secretary, said to me: 'Would you care for a piece of chocolate cake?' I said: 'I'd love chocolate cake.' Off he went and came back with this huge chunk of chocolate cake. By this time the Queen Mother was chatting to me, and I was presented with this large hunk of very gooey chocolate cake. I thought: 'This is going to be difficult. Do I balance it until the conversation is finished, or am I supposed to nibble it in between times while she is speaking to me?' And again I saw this twinkle. She must have realised my discomfort, and she said: 'I have to apologise for the cake, if you find any of the chocolate buttons missing, or any finger prints. You see we had it made specially for my daughter coming yesterday, and she didn't eat any of it. She just sat and picked the chocolate buttons off.' And that was the Queen she was talking about.

At the end of the evening, as we were going off, Sir Martin Gilliat said: 'You'll have a piece of cake to take home.' We were all coming down the main staircase and the Queen Mother came down part of the way with us. Various people in the party were carrying our instruments and things, and as the Queen Mother waved goodbye she said: 'We must do this again soon.' Then she said: 'David, you must pipe everybody out.' So David had to get his pipes back out of the case, and play all the way down the stairs and out to the front door. Then Sir Martin Gilliat came rushing up with this napkin with a big hunk of chocolate cake in it for me. 'You have forgotten your bit of cake.' I thought it was hilarious. It was a lovely evening, and a lovely memory to have because it was such fun.

Mrs Christian Bell

Widow of the former Minister of Canisbay Church, near the Castle of Mey, and a regular guest of the Queen Mother.

It was 1958 when we came to live up here, and when she came on holiday we met her. I remember the first time we were invited to the castle for afternoon tea. It was a very thrilling experience, and a little bit nerve-racking, but the Queen Mother made you feel so much at home that you weren't many minutes there before you were quite relaxed. After that we always went in August and sometimes in October. We would get a telephone call inviting us, and it was always just us, plus the people staying at the castle. When you came away you would feel marvellous. My husband used to say: 'That is the batteries recharged for another year.' That's the effect she has on you.

My husband is dead now, but I still get invited. It's very kind of the Queen Mother to still think about me. Happiness just seems to flow from her. She is so full of fun, and bright and lively. She loves young people and she is very young at heart herself.

We talk about all sorts of interests, and people she has known previously. She likes to keep up with what's going on, and I am usually able to supply all the local gossip. She gets the *John O'Groats Journal* at Clarence House, so that keeps her up to date as well.

When my husband was the Minister she used to discuss what went on in church – the sermon, the hymns and the psalms. When we went for dinner, she would say she liked a particular one but perhaps knew it sung to a different tune. She took great interest in all that went on in the church and church life, and she supported it by sending gifts every year.

Quite sincerely, I should say she is one of the dearest people I have ever met. She was so kind and caring when my husband was ill. She visited him, and kept in touch with the hospital all the time to find out how he was progressing. He had been paralysed. She came to visit him and sent him flowers, and sent a representative to his funeral.

When he died she was a tremendous support to me. I had a telegram from her the next day, and then I met her a month or two afterwards when she came up to the castle. She talked to me quite a lot about him, and how much she appreciated his church work and enjoyed having him at the castle. I am sure she realised exactly how I felt, because she had experienced the same thing, at a much younger age too. She never spoke about her own bereavement, but she had a very sad expression when she was talking about my husband, which I am sure must have been a reflection of her sorrow at her own husband's death.

She was also very kind in helping us with the house I live in now. When my husband retired we had to leave the house we were in. We looked around lots of places, but we couldn't find anywhere that was available, not even a council house. We knew the Queen Mother had bought this house when she bought the surrounding land, so we asked her if we might have a loan of it for a year or two until we found something else. She said she

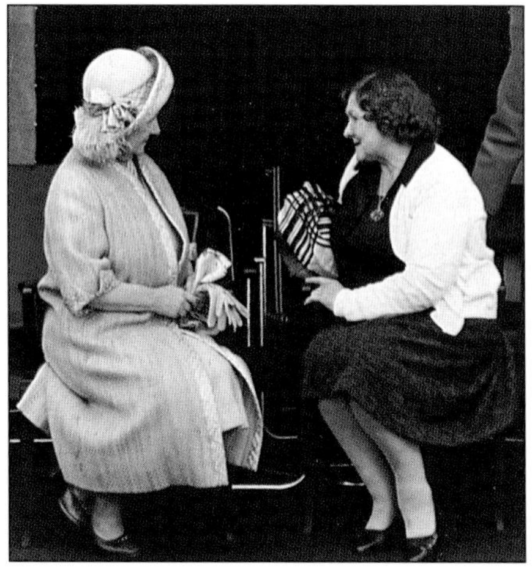

The Queen Mother and
Mrs Christian Bell.

would be delighted and she had it all done up for us. It was completely reconstructed inside and had new windows put in. It's beautiful, and lovely and warm. We were both very grateful to Her Majesty for this great gesture. My husband and I were very happy for the two years he was able to be there, and Queen Elizabeth used to pop in and see him, which was very uplifting for him when he was so ill. Sometimes she brought him a book and they discussed bird-life and lots of things they had in common. He always cheered up the day she came.

I think she loves Caithness because it is completely different from any other of her other residences. The fact, too, that it is actually her own must also give her a great sense of ownership. The panoramic view from the castle with big wide seascapes and landscapes, and rocks and seals and islands is marvellous. It's so open and free compared with cities, and the air is so fresh and bracing. After all the duties that she performs, she comes here for a well-earned rest, and we all appreciate that and respect her privacy. We love to see her, but we don't buzz round her or try to make her feel that she is being encompassed by peering people.

We have some marvellous sunsets here, with the sun going right down over Dunnet Head. I can remember one occasion when after dinner she said: 'I think we'll go up onto the top of the castle tonight and have a look at the view and the sunset.' It was breathtaking up there, and we stood for quite a long time watching the sun going down. It was quite exhilarating.

I look upon her as a woman of very deep faith, and I think no matter what has happened in her lifetime – and she has had vicissitudes in life as we all have – she seems to have been able to surmount it all. I put it down to her faith and to the fact that she must realise how loved she is by so many people. They love her, admire her and are loyal to her, and I think she is probably aware of the great volume of prayers that are said for her. Combined with all this, she has such a joyful character, and is so full of fun and laughter that it makes her an absolutely unique person.

The Reverend Alex Muir

Minister at Canisbay Church, near the Castle of Mey.

When I was told about the church I had no idea that she was one of the congregation. My interest is in the church, and nothing to do with her being in the vicinity and coming to church from time to time. But it is a privilege to be able to minister to the Queen Mother. She is a very special person, and one comes to love her very much.

A word often used of her is gracious. I don't mean she's pious or formal, but gracious in a sparkly, human way – a combination of great humanity and kindness, and an interest in other people. When she is speaking to a person, that person is important to her, which makes them feel at ease and draws a response from them.

Her visits to the church are quite informal; she is a very easy-going person. She arrives by car and I see her into the church. There are always tourists with cameras who take snaps of her coming into the church. She comes in the front door, not the private entrance at the rear, and the congregation stands as she enters. She smiles, of course, and I take her to her pew, which faces the pulpit. Then I go to the pulpit and begin the service. The atmosphere is very reverent and, in a sense, ordinary. We are there to worship God, and the Queen Mother is a worshipper with us. She is behind the congregation, not sitting at the front, so she is not seen by everybody.

Afterwards there are people outside again, taking pictures and sometimes making comments. There was one tourist who asked for a photograph to be taken with her. I don't know how he managed it, and it has only happened once.

She has a very strong and genuine faith, which I'm sure has been a great support to her. She loves to worship God. When she comes to church she always has her Bible with the place

The Reverend Alex Muir beside the Queen Mother
in typical Caithness weather.

marked for the reading, and always wants to know what the readings are going to be before the service. She looks up the scripture passage with me, and as I read she is reading as well. When the equerry phones to say she is coming, perhaps on a Saturday or Friday night, he also asks what the hymns are. She brings her own hymn book.

We do discuss religious matters from time to time – the condition of the church and so on, and interest in the country generally in the faith of Jesus Christ. I don't want to say too much about it – I think it's a private matter.

The major difference when she comes to church is the visitors and tourists. This church isn't well attended by tourists – it's some way from John O'Groats – but when the Queen Mum is due to come, the word gets around and we have a lot more visitors that day. So there are more people and the singing is better.

My lasting memory will be of sitting next to her at dinner in the Castle of Mey, and seeing her smile.

Mrs Joan Webster

Housekeeper and wife of the gardener at the Castle of Mey.

Over the winter I just look after the house – just general maintenance. From the end of May though, I start getting ready for the Court coming, for Queen Elizabeth's visit. You do just a normal spring clean like any other housewife would do. I have got three ladies that come in and help every year, at the beginning of June. She is usually here for three and a half weeks in August, and comes back again sometimes for a week in October.

We talk about things like the personal likes or dislikes of the guests, or where you should put a certain person, which bedroom they will have and things like that. She tells you if this person wants a particular drink, that maybe we don't generally serve, or a little vase of flowers for this lady, or a certain book for this gentleman.

Queen Elizabeth takes a lot of personal interest in the rooms because it is her house. Right from the very start she has picked all her drapes and cottons and bed covers and that sort of thing. She also takes an interest in us as a family. My husband is the gardener and our two children have been brought up here. They were only two and three-and-a-half when we arrived here. She has seen them grow up, and has followed their progress, and she always asks about them and their husbands and wives. And now we have grandchildren she takes an interest in them, and we have been asked to bring them up so that she can meet them. You don't expect that of somebody like Queen Elizabeth, who is way above us, in a sense.

She cares about everybody. She is concerned if she sees a disaster on the television, as well as about us and her own family.

Mr and Mrs Webster, the gardener and the housekeeper at the Castle of Mey.

Ashe Windham

Former equerry to the Queen Mother. One of her younger friends, he continued to be invited to stay after he had left her service.

I was a friend of a great-nephew of hers, called Mikey. He was Lord Glamis in those days, but he's now the Earl of Strathmore. We'd been to prep school together and then Eton, and when we left, he was asked by the Queen Mother whether he'd like to go and stay up at the Castle of Mey. As it was his first time up there she said: 'Well, do bring a friend,' and I was lucky enough to be the only person who wasn't actually doing anything else in August. So I went up there at the age of eighteen. I was very nervous. I remember driving down the long drive, with beautiful trees – about the only ones in Caithness – at the bottom of it, and we swept round and were greeted by barking corgis and the figure of Queen Elizabeth. She immediately put one at ease. That is the marvellous thing about her – she's got a tremendous ability to put anybody at their ease. She could just look at them and people would feel at home. We had a chat – she's very interested in Eton and goes there two or three times a year, and much enjoys visiting the Provost, Lord Charteris, who is the Queen's former Private Secretary. She tells the story of arriving at Eton for some very important opening of the school hall, and she saw this great placard by the railings saying GOOD QUEEN MUM SACK MCCRUM, who happened to be the headmaster at the time. Mr McCrum left in the normal course of events three or four years later, so their wishes weren't carried out, but she thought that was very amusing.

Later on I became her equerry. I was serving in the Irish Guards when I was appointed to the job. It really was a peculiar job in many ways, because you're working for the Queen Mother in the morning, and working for the regiment in the afternoon. I used to get in about half past nine, review any mail that had arrived overnight, perhaps write one or two letters, and generally organise all her travel arrangements. Woe betide you if you got them wrong, although she'd never be nasty enough to tick you off publicly. In fact everything works so perfectly, and the chauffeurs know so precisely what happens year to year, that you don't actually make mistakes, but she certainly took a keen interest. She is very good if anything does go wrong. For instance, the Royal Flight helicopter came down in Windsor Great Park with engine failure when she was on it. She was completely unflappable, and got straight back into the replacement helicopter which was sent to land alongside the broken-down one. She loves flying by helicopter, and thoroughly enjoys the excitement of it. She takes everything in her stride.

Another much publicised event was when a fish bone lodged in her throat during dinner. She said: 'I'm quite all right; I'll just retire to my room.' Luckily Princess Margaret was there and was able to say: 'We think we ought to do something about it,' and after some delay the doctor was summoned. She was rushed off to hospital and had an operation, but she would never have gone on her own account. She wasn't in the least bit worried. Minor infirmities she shrugs aside completely. Even in the wilds of North Scotland she's out with the dogs two or three times a day. I remember some years ago she had a bit of a cold, but there was no holding back at all. She is a famous sight in Caithness, down by the sea wrapped up from head to toe, with a great blue scarf pulled tightly round her ears in a howling gale, and two corgis obediently trotting along behind. She loves it up there at the Castle of Mey. It's a beautiful place which looks right onto the Orkneys, and on a clear day you can see fifteen or twenty miles. It's always changing; the light is different, and there are wonderful shadows on the sea from the scudding clouds.

When she is at Birkhall almost every day you'll go down to her log cabin for a picnic lunch by the river, which is substantial by any standards. You probably start off with something fishy, like a mousse, and then usually a bit of cold ham or cold grouse, which might have been shot the day before. This is followed up

Ashe Windham, a regular guest at the Castle of Mey, with the Queen Mother in Caithness.

by the traditional jam tarts produced by the cook. There is a great joke because Queen Elizabeth insists on people chopping off the top and filling it with cream, and then you've got to try and manoeuvre this into your mouth without getting cream everywhere. The old hands put a drop or two in the bottom, but the enthusiastic beginners fill it up to the top and suffer the consequences.

There is a very amusing fishing story that she tells. One day she appeared on the river bank and there was somebody fishing on the opposite side, a lady clad in breast-high waders and fishing down the pool. She was fairly well into the pool when she spotted the Queen Mother on the other side, and immediately stooped into a low curtsey, whereupon her waders filled with water and she all but floated down the river. When Queen Elizabeth tells that story she always sounds shocked that somebody should get so wet on her account. She is someone who will always see the lighter side of things; never one to dwell on the darker bits. She loves recounting what's happened during the day and having a good laugh at it afterwards; not in any sense maliciously, but anything amusing is always made a great thing of.

Usually after dinner at the Castle of Mey we sit down and play a game of Racing Demon, at which she's an absolute expert. The great joke is that Queen Elizabeth always wins; partly because she's brilliant at it – you need to be very quick and have an awful lot of skill – but also because the guests are rather worried about perhaps catching the midnight train down to the south, if they win too regularly. Alternatively, somebody will either turn on the record player or play the piano, and we'll have an impromptu eightsome reel on the carpet, which doesn't make it any easier. There's also someone called Hetty Munro who lives in Thurso and who organises ceilidhs. Queen Elizabeth heard about this and said it would be great fun to have a Caithness ceilidh at the castle. So about once a year it's become a fairly well-established event. They come in after dinner, and sing songs and play musical instruments, and it's always a very amusing evening.

I think she enjoys Scotland because she can be more relaxed about what she does. Picking flowers and that sort of thing. One evening I remember particularly. We'd come back from the Queen's log cabin at Balmoral and we'd had an interesting dinner cooked by the Prince of Wales. I think it was venison which had got fairly tough, and Queen Elizabeth is not a great enjoyer of venison. As I was driving Queen Elizabeth back in the Land Rover, she leant over and said: 'Ashe, are you feeling a little bit hungry?' and I said: 'No, not really, Ma'am.' She said: 'Well, I am. I think we'll make some scrambled eggs when we get back to Birkhall.' I remember we all trooped off into the kitchen and I was No. 1 on the toast. Queen Elizabeth was cracking the eggs into a basin and much whisking was going on, and shortly after midnight we had a great plate of scrambled eggs on toast.

I will always think of her as a person who radiates charm, who makes you feel immediately at your ease, and who is tremendous fun to be with. There are many occasions when one's life has been brightened immeasurably by the presence of Queen Elizabeth. She has a memory for faces and names that has astounded people she's met perhaps fifteen or twenty years previously. She goes straight up to them and says: 'Hello Mr So-and-So.' They beam all over; it makes them feel very special. She is not prompted by her staff, as some people might think. I don't know how she does it, but it makes people realise that she truly is interested.

Politicians

From 1923, when she became Duchess of York, through her years as Queen, and finally during the decades after the King's death, the Queen Mother met almost every major figure in public life.

King George VI and Queen Elizabeth on their way to the State Opening of Parliament in 1937, after the Abdication. From then on, the Queen Mother knew every prime minister and many of the members of their cabinets.

Lord Home of The Hirsel

Former Conservative Foreign Secretary and Prime Minister, he was Parliamentary Private Secretary to Neville Chamberlain at the time of his negotiations with Hitler in 1938. A member of another great Scottish family, Lord Home knew the Queen Mother for well over sixty years.

I must have met Queen Elizabeth first in the twenties. I went to Glamis to play cricket. Her parents were a very attractive couple to a young man. They were a very large family, so the young got a good look in, and we had a splendid time on that visit. Glamis itself was the centre of an agricultural estate, and I think that Lord and Lady Strathmore, and Queen Elizabeth and the whole family knew all the tenants very well. They used to be part of the local scene in anything that was going on, so there was an enormously charming and friendly atmosphere. Queen Elizabeth was brought up a country girl, in a large family, and no doubt took the buffeting that the youngest daughter would get from brothers and sisters.

Her Scottish country upbringing must have had a lasting influence, because she walks the hills like few people one has seen. She understands all about the country and the farms, the horses and the dogs. She's also a very good fisherman. All those country pursuits come naturally. I always notice two things about Queen Elizabeth; her extraordinary vitality that has lasted right through her life, and her natural sympathy with people. It doesn't matter who it is, she seems to get on to their wavelength straight away, and make them feel at ease. Her ability to talk to everybody in that way must have come from her early family life, and moving around the estate and the country. In the twenties the main thing I remember about her was her vitality. It really struck one all the time. Wherever she was she wholeheartedly threw herself into whatever was happening, and obviously enjoyed it. There was always a smile and a ready word for everybody. That is how life ought to be, and everybody is drawn into enjoying it with her.

She is a strong character too. When Edward VIII abdicated, it must have taken a very strong character to deal with that situation as the Queen Mother did. It was a time of turmoil, and the whole sense of values of the British people was upset, because nobody had anticipated that such a situation could arise. Queen Elizabeth brought good humour and a poise which steadied everybody down. She greatly reinforced the new King, and I think her contribution was very important at that time. It was necessary to restore confidence in the monarchy and the constitutional position of the King. Queen Elizabeth contributed to this in a way that probably nobody else could have done.

Lord Home with the Queen Mother
at St Paul's Walden Bury.

It was after the war that I really got to know her. I used to go and stay with her up on Deeside and we had some very happy parties up there. And I got to know her in London too. It was always a very happy experience to watch her doing public functions. She is very dignified and at the same time has a word for everybody. After all these years of entertaining in Buckingham Palace and elsewhere, she knows a lot of the world's characters and personalities. As a hostess at somewhere like Birkhall she's marvellously good. No fussiness or anything like that, but she's always very attentive to the needs of guests and their peculiarities. It's fun, a country-house-party atmosphere. I remember I used to go when there were a lot of grouse in Scotland, so we used to shoot grouse. She doesn't herself shoot, but she loved it, and used to come out with the guns. In the evenings you would play various games after dinner. I remember once when Lord Salisbury was staying there and we were playing Old Maid, the game when you're left with a queen, and she said: 'Oh, Bobbety [Lord Salisbury], how are you getting on? You don't look very happy.' And he said: 'Oh, Ma'am, I've been left with three howwible, howwible queens.' He never had an 'r' in his vocabulary. And she said: 'Oh, Bobbety, I don't think that's a very good way of putting it, do you?' There was always lots of laughter.

She is quite tireless; she must have very good health. I think part of that is very good digestion, and lots of walking too. Regular exercise in hill country does help. I always feel a new man when I get back to the Border hills. On one occasion I remember staying with her sister-in-law down at St Paul's Walden Bury in Hertfordshire. We'd had a very long day, and she'd had an even longer one because there was a Red Cross fête. When we got to twelve o'clock at night we were all gasping and wondering when she was going to go to bed, when she suddenly said: 'Wouldn't it be a good idea to have a square dance out on the stones in front of the drawing room there.' So we all went out and square-danced till about two in the morning. Absolutely tireless.

Lord Hailsham

Son of a Lord Chancellor, he was close to affairs of state from an early age. He became an MP in 1938, and held many government posts, including the Lord Chancellorship like his father. He was a regular guest of the Queen Mother during weekends at Royal Lodge, Windsor.

Following her engagement to the Duke of York there was a great wedding in 1923 in Westminster Abbey, which was just as important in its own way – except there was no television – as a wedding of that sort would be now. My father talked to me quite a lot about the new Duchess of York. He said how wonderful she was and how she'd been very afraid of the role that she was going to have to play, although at that time it didn't involve being queen. People said she was rather hesitant about it – this was the sort of thing my father would say at the breakfast table. It was a formidable thing to be in the public eye to that extent – to be the wife of the younger brother of the person who was going to be king. She was very highly born in the Scottish aristocracy, but she wasn't a royal in the ordinary sense of the word, and she was quite young at the time. I don't think they gave much thought to the possibility of ever being king and queen. I think they put it out of their minds if it did occur to them. King George V predicted it, or predicted that King Edward VIII, as he subsequently became, wouldn't be a great success. My memory of the Abdication is simply a small personal snapshot. I was the heir to a Viscountcy and it was the first time, and one of the very few times when, as the heir to a peerage, I sat on the steps of the throne. I heard the actual declaration there on a very dark December day, I remember. The Abdication was a convulsion. It had never happened since

Richard II. James II theoretically abdicated, but he didn't abdicate in the same sense Edward VIII did. He ran away.

Queen Elizabeth became Queen and was dedicated from the first to the monarchical institution, as something more than a single crowned head. Of course the crowned head is the centre-piece, and without it the rest wouldn't exist, but I think she is devoted to the whole monarchical conception of our social and national life. She feels it is essential to the nation with every fibre of her being. Her role at that time was crucial. King George VI needed a great deal of support. He didn't relish the role of becoming a monarch out of turn, so to speak. He realised it was his duty, but he had this considerable impediment in his speech, and therefore the support she gave him was, I think, crucial to the success which he undoubtedly made of the monarchy. I don't think anyone could have done a better job than she did. It was just one of those things which was providential.

Her qualities are really too numerous to list, but I would put two, I think, highest. First of all is her vitality, from youth to what in most people would be old age. Her vital, sparkling character comes across every time she appears in public or private. The other thing is that when she is talking to you, and I mean by that to anyone, she gives the impression, which I think is not just put on, that she is more interested in you than anybody else in the world. When you meet royalty, whether it is the Queen or a royal duchess or a minor prince, it is rather a formidable social occasion for the subject, the ordinary commoner, or even a member of the House of Lords. You are definitely a little shy, but she puts you at your ease. I think it is simply that she genuinely likes people, is interested in them and in the same things that they are interested in. She has a great humanity. It's not at all false, not just a performance, but an art form, as well as a deeply felt and sincere way of behaving, which reflects the character of the person. Nor is it done without effort; nothing that is worth doing is done without effort and conscious application.

Another great quality is her courage which I think is essential to her make up. To face the crisis that she had to face when she became Queen Consort, and then to have to face the war and the bombing – Buckingham Palace itself was bombed – showed enormous courage. I would rate the King and Queen's importance at that time very highly indeed, because they were stable, they were relaxed to all appearances, and they were supportive. They went to the places where people were suffering, and were well received, and spoke to the people whose homes had been blown up. The monarchical institution operated by that married couple was a very important factor in keeping public opinion united and firm, and determined to go on. After all, on paper we had lost the war in 1940, and it was only a matter of time. But nobody would accept this and they didn't accept it either. They symbolised the continuity of family life, and though at the top of the social tree, they remained exactly what ordinary families are, a loving husband, a loving and supportive wife, and adoring children.

I'm very pleased to have got to know Queen Elizabeth over the years. You can't be a Privy Councillor for as long as I have, and hold some of the ancient offices of State, like Lord President or Chancellor or Lord Privy Seal, without getting to know the Royal Family on fairly relaxed social terms, without in any way presuming. I mean the thing that one must never do with those people, who are entitled to their privacy, is to presume in any way. But for instance, whenever there is a State banquet the old offices like Lord Chancellor and Lord Privy Seal and Lord President are asked as guests, and they are probably placed between two members of the Royal Family. I have always found that Queen Elizabeth is very ready to talk to anyone about all the things which interest her, as long as she trusts you not to break confidence; and that can be anything – whatever is in the headlines that week. She is a lady of strongly-held convictions and beliefs. She has a very strong sense of public duty and private duty, and of the difference between right and wrong. I believe her to be a Christian, as I am myself, and she never deviates from that. Not that she doesn't enjoy herself; she likes fun, games, laughter, and songs. She likes the ordinary good things of life.

Lord Callaghan

The only man ever to hold all four offices, he was Labour Home Secretary, Chancellor of the Exchequer, Foreign Secretary and Prime Minister. His political eminence brought him into contact with the Queen Mother on many occasions.

I think what stands out most about Queen Elizabeth is her enthusiasm – the fact that whatever job she's doing she shows tremendous interest in everybody who's engaged in it. In her general understanding of the British people, she's a master, or should I say a mistress. She is the kind of person who is naturally interested in others, and also the kind of person who has immense high spirits. She doesn't need anyone to raise them all the time; she raises the spirits of others. I think she has an extraordinary natural touch with everybody in this country; no matter who they are, she can make them feel at ease as soon as they meet her. She makes them feel that she's interested in what they're doing. She has a great sense of noblesse oblige, that is to say, she really feels that the Crown has a responsibility to embrace the whole of the people of the United Kingdom. She feels they are 'her' people.

She is a person who regards every morning as a new challenge and a day that she's really going to set out to enjoy. She really skips around the place. I know that is true; I've seen her skip on one or two occasions, literally skip across the room, even when she was getting quite old. She is a person of great natural enthusiasm and she infects others with the same enthusiasm. She is entirely uninhibited and lacks any kind of pomposity or affectation. I remember when the vacancy fell for the Lord Warden of the Cinque Ports, those frontline towns in Kent that withstood the Battle of Britain and the possibilities of invasion. I discussed the vacancy with the present Queen and she very kindly said:

'Well, why don't you take it?' But I said I didn't think it was quite right, certainly at that stage of my life. I said I thought the Queen Mother was appropriate because she and the King had been so much in the battle at the time of the Second World War. So she said: 'Well, you ask her.' We were at Balmoral, and after we'd been to church on the Sunday morning, we were having a drink before luncheon and the Queen said to the Queen Mother: 'The Prime Minister wants to have a word with you; why don't you go into the library?' So we went into the library, and I said to the Queen Mother that I thought it would be most appropriate if she would agree to be Lord Warden of the Cinque Ports, because of the natural connection with the war and so on. And she put her hand on her heart, as she does, and she said: 'I'm so relieved. I thought you had me in here because I'd said something wrong and you were going to reprove me.' It's that kind of natural reaction, so unexpected, that makes you very fond of her indeed.

Another thing, she can be awfully indiscreet. I remember when the European Community had only nine members, and the Queen very kindly invited all the European heads of state and all the rest of us to dinner. It was a very small dinner party, only about twenty people sitting round the table. I was sitting next to the Queen Mother, and there was a slight lull in the conversation and she turned to me and she said: 'I do think it's so good that we've joined the community, don't you?' I said: 'Well, yes, of course, but why particularly?' 'Well,' she said in a rather loud, piercing voice, with all the others sitting there, 'you know, we can teach them so much, can't we?' I said: 'Ssshhh.' 'Well,' she said, 'we can, can't we?' She insisted on it, at which the conversation took off again. It's that kind of thing that endeared her to me.

I also remember that she was very kind to Michael Foot when the press complained about the coat he wore at the Cenotaph. It was before he got into trouble, not after, and she spoke to him very naturally about it, and I think it was something she meant because she always puts people at their ease. He'd worn this coat – it wasn't a donkey jacket as was reported – which was perhaps an unconventional coat, but perfectly respectable, and she said to him: 'What a sensible thing to wear. I wish I could do it myself!' I thought this was extremely kind of her.

Lord Callaghan.

There is a complete lack of pomposity about her, and a desire to make people feel at home and to embrace everybody. You would never hear her referring to any section of the community as being enemies of the country; she regards them all – whether they are miners or fishermen, of high rank or low rank – as part of her people. This, I think, is the great strength of the Crown, that she could give a feeling to people that everyone matters to her and that she does care about them. I suppose it is a slightly old-fashioned view, but she has old-fashioned virtues and they are none the worse for that.

Lord Carrington

Conservative Foreign Secretary (1979–82). Secretary-General of NATO (1984–88). He became chairman of Christie's in 1988. An unstuffy aristocrat, he was a friend and weekend guest of the Queen Mother for many years.

She loves the Commonwealth and everything to do with it, and because she does they all love her. If she has a favourite, I would suspect it is Canada, but don't tell the Australians. There is a very strong feeling of British Empire turned into British Commonwealth. I think she feels very strongly that it is a sort of brotherhood, regardless of colour, that there is a family, and that she's part of it. The fact that she still goes to Canada in the middle of the summer, which would exhaust most people who were thirty years younger, is partly a sense of obligation and partly a love of Canada. Also because she still has this enormous interest in what is going on in the world, and in seeing things develop over the years she has known it.

She was of vital importance to Britain itself at the time of the Abdication. I was at school and I remember very clearly – it was the days before you were allowed your own radio at that school – that we were shepherded into a room to hear the Duke of Windsor's Abdication speech. I don't think one was really conscious, apart from the headlines, of the great constitutional crisis that might have arisen. Looking back one can see that she was of the most vital importance. After all, it might all have gone very wrong, and I think that it was her personality that saw it all through. Obviously the King as well, but he was much shyer and more withdrawn to begin with. I think her part is very much recognised by the British people, even if they don't remember all that. The same is true of the example that she set during the war. That was a marvellous thing for the British people.

When Buckingham Palace was bombed, I think it made everybody feel that it wasn't just the East End of London that was taking it, though it was taking the brunt. There were other people, who were in a more privileged position, who were running the same sort of dangers. There was never any suggestion of pulling out and going somewhere safe; they were all part of it like we were at that time. I think Queen Elizabeth has a very strong sense of duty or obligation. Once in that position of being Queen, which I imagine she would never have wanted to be in, she felt an enormous obligation to carry out her duty as well and as conscientiously as anybody could carry it out. Over the years she has probably found it very rewarding because of the affection of everybody she meets, but at the beginning it must have been hard work. It is quite extraordinary, you see people's faces change as they watch her passing in a car.

She has got an enormous sense of humour and fun, and a sense of the ridiculous. When we meet she wants to know the background to what's going on in international affairs, but she also likes a bit of gossip. When I was in Brussels she would want to know all about the heads of government meetings – who said what and what they were like and so on. More seriously though, she would want to know what the problems are. Everything about her is of a whole, not just serious or just fun. Of course, she is very well-informed. After all, you can't be in that position and meet everybody in the world without being pretty well-informed. She will also pick you up if you're wrong, and say: 'That wasn't right. I remember I was there, actually.'

When you first meet her she is absolutely marvellous. Everybody's a bit nervous, but she's so easy and so interesting. When you read all the superlatives in the press and hear the things that people tell you about her, you think they simply can't be true. But the fact is, they are true. She is exactly as she seems to be. She's not a sugar-plum fairy; she has very definite opinions, about things and about people, but is also the most charming person you have ever met. It is natural, not put on.

I remember once when we were staying at Royal Lodge, it was a very wet Sunday afternoon and my wife and I went out for a walk with Queen Elizabeth into the Saville Gardens. She was just in gumboots and mackintosh and a hat, with a couple of corgis. There were only two other people in the garden and they did a double-take. They circled round her and said: 'It can't be, just can't be ... it is.' And she said quite firmly: 'It is,' and then spent twenty minutes charming them with her naturalness and interest in them, and the fact that they were there and what they were doing. You couldn't be uncaptivated by her.

We have been lucky enough to be asked to Royal Lodge in the summer over the years, and it is something one looks forward to enormously because it is such fun. It is the most unstuffy thing that you can imagine. There are a lot of other people there who are friends, and there is a splendid routine, but in another sense you never know what is going to happen; for instance after dinner on Saturday night she will sometimes dance reels. It is just like staying in a country house, with the dogs and tea out on the terrace, not at all as you would imagine a sort of stuffy weekend. One has been to much stuffier weekends in other people's houses. They aren't like that when you go to Royal Lodge. You find yourself singing 'My Old Man Said Follow The Van' or something like that. Quite often Quintin Hailsham is there and he's got a splendid rendering in execrable French of the *Marseillaise*, which he sings at the top of his voice after dinner, rather tunelessly. It's become a sort of institution, actually. Of course, you always go to church in the Royal Chapel on a Sunday morning, and quite often somebody has forgotten to shut the dogs in and they arrive in the chapel too, and have to be shut out with a great deal of hoo-ha. It is all very natural and ordinary.

I will remember her as the most graceful person I've ever met, and the most captivating, because she combines in one person so many different qualities, knowledge and interest and charm and determination. All those things which, taken as a whole, make a rather remarkable person.

PICTURE CREDITS

Camera Press 28, 36, 42 (top), 43 (bottom), 44, 57, 62, 69, 70–71, 195, 252; Tim Graham Picture Library 66, 188–189; Hulton Getty Collection 20, 23, 26, 29, 31 (top), 33, 35, 42 (bottom), 51, 60, 63, 127, 131, 197, 209; Anwar Hussein Picture Library 61; Illustrated London News 5, 14, 15, 16–17, 47, 48, 52, 55; Derry Moore 107; Popperfoto 12, 134–135; Press Association 168, 183, 191; Rex Features 64; Syndication International 17 (left), 27, 31 (bottom), 43 (top), 50, 101, 148–149, 156, 202–203, 206, 216–217, 237, 242; Topham Picture Library 38–39, 82; Universal Pictorial Press 89, 177.

Plates

Camera Press picture dates 1902, 1907×2, 1922, 1923, (Cecil Beaton 1948, 1956, 1950s 1970×3), (Richard Open 1986), (Lord Snowdon 1987), Anthony Crickmay 1990×2 portraits), (Lord Snowdon 1997), (Anthony Crickmay 1997); Tim Graham 1978, 1980, 1982, 1984, 1985, 1990, 1994; Hulton Getty 1936, 1940s, 1941×2, 1962, 1968.

All other photographs courtesy the contributors.